Black & Gold Party Gras

New Orleans' Championship Celebration in Pictures

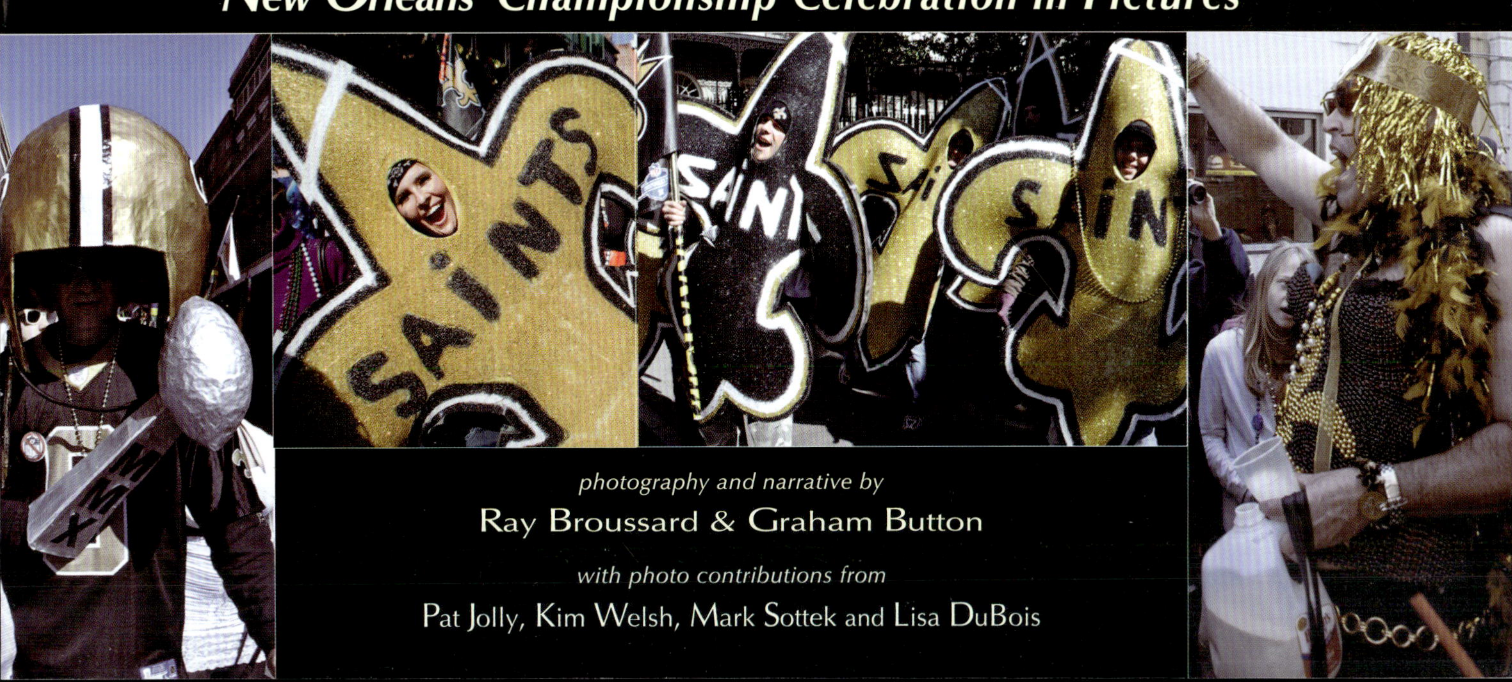

photography and narrative by

Ray Broussard & Graham Button

with photo contributions from

Pat Jolly, Kim Welsh, Mark Sottek and Lisa DuBois

Grab somebody, come on down
Bring a paintbrush, we're painting the town
There's some sweetness goin' 'round
Dreams do come true in New Orleans

—"Down in New Orleans (Finale)"
from the soundtrack (released Nov. 23, 2009)
to the animated feature *The Princess and the Frog*
(words and music by Randy Newman)

Library of Congress-in-Publishing Date
Broussard, Ray and Button, Graham
Black & Gold Party Gras
ISBN: 978-0-615-41581-9
Printed in China

The victory party on Bourbon Street after the game.

Photo galleries and more at
www.BlackandGoldPartyGras.com

Introduction

Saints play-by-play announcer Jim Henderson, who in August 2009 predicted a championship for New Orleans, called Super Bowl XLIV on WWL Radio (AM870). "Get ready to party with the Lombardi, New Orleans!" he rejoiced, as the final seconds ticked off the clock in the Saints' momentous 31 - 17 victory over the Indianapolis Colts.

Moments later, the game's MVP, Drew Brees, was radiant in the Vince Lombardi Trophy presentation ceremony. With a sterling silver Tiffany football in hand, the Saints quarterback and team leader—who came to New Orleans as if in a fairy-tale fantasy and helped galvanize an urban-renewal movement—reflected on the glorious convergence of a Saints championship and the city's most distinctive civic ritual.

"Mardi Gras may never end," he said with a smile.

No question: The collective mania known as Mardi Gras Madness was about to acquire a whole new meaning. The most jubilant party ever in America's most celebrated party town had begun with a resounding bang. *Who Dat!*

That the Who Dat Nation—famous for rambunctious fanfare—was uniquely well equipped to celebrate the historic moment in the biggest way possible was never in doubt. For in the realm of revelry and creative self-expression—dance, spirit songs, costumes, decorative regalia and homemade signs—the Who Dats reign supreme.

Sure, the Raider Nation has its share of colorful, swashbuckling characters that look as if they just stepped off the set of a *Mad Max* movie or sci-fi pirate adventure. But fans of the Oakland Raiders are a notoriously abrasive lot, reveling in a "bad boy" image and given to taunting fans of visiting teams.

By contrast, when fans of opposing teams come to New Orleans for games, they walk away feeling like they passed a good time, win or lose. Explains Keith Twitchell, president of the Committee for a Better New Orleans and a keen observer of the city's folkways: "We combine absolutely rabid Saints fanaticism with grace, Southern hospitality and, obviously, centuries of experience at partying."

However one chooses to define it, the hoopla surrounding the Saints says a lot about what makes New Orleans so weird and wonderful. Certainly, no other place on Earth could have spawned the phenomenon the local media dubbed "Who Dat hysteria."

The term "Who Dat," with roots in African American musical variety theater dating back to the late 1800s, had long been a popular rallying cry of Saints fans. Now it had become a catchphrase for the over-the-top frenzy inspired by the winning ways of a team with a long history of struggling to reward the devotion bestowed upon it. Mardi Gras 2010 would bear witness to the Who Dat Nation in the thrall of ecstatic redemption.

Sometimes a theme just begs to be milked for all it's worth. Such was the case with Hurricane Katrina at Mardi Gras 2006, and so it was again with the Saints.

Six months after levee failures nearly wiped out the city, Mardi Gras offered a respite from the trauma of loss and displacement, as well as a cathartic forum for channeling frustration and delivering satirical commentary through costuming and parade themes. It was also an opportunity to make a statement to the world: We're here; the city is open for business and can handle a big event; and we will honor and preserve the traditions we hold dear.

Four years later, Mardi Gras presented an opportunity to not only celebrate the Saints but also make an affirmative statement about the city's recovery and what Mardi Gras and the true "spirit of New Orleans" were all about. Often associated in the popular imagination with mass inebriation and immodest exhibitionism, Mardi Gras is really more about an entire community coming together and drawing on a range of art forms to revel with inimitable panache.

For a citizenry so exceptionally well practiced in the art of diversion, having the climax of Carnival come on the heels of a World Championship seemed more like a holy blessing than a fortuitous coincidence. For if the triumph of the Saints was destiny, as Brees himself believed—"it was all meant to be" he said in the Lombardi ceremony—then so, too, was the happy proximity of the Super Bowl to Fat Tuesday.

Even the most grizzled veterans of high times in the Crescent City had to pinch themselves. Could it possibly get any better than this? Get me in dat number, cher—and throw me something black and gold, mister!

At the Superdome in May 2010, Drew Brees delivered the Loyola University commencement address. Relating how a shoulder injury that put his career on the line turned out to be a blessing in disguise because it brought him to New Orleans, the civic savior and gridiron wizard urged his audience to see adversity as an opportunity.

The confluence of Carnival and a Saints Super Bowl unleashed a Category 5 outpouring of Who Dat pride and do-it-yourself artistry. Danielle Brutsche created this shoebox-size float, entitled *Day of the Death of the Aints*, for the 'tit Rex "micro parade" ("'tit" is an abbreviation of "petit"). The procession of handcrafted miniature floats rolled through the Bywater neighborhood on the eve of the Super Bowl.

Membership in the Divine Protectors of Endangered Pleasures, aka the Divas—a flamboyant, Mardi Gras-esque version of a quilting bee—is predicated in part upon crafting an elaborately adorned bustier. On the Friday before Mardi Gras, a vivacious black-and-gold contingent led their French Quarter promenade—channeling the spirit of the moment as New Orleans reveled in its first-ever Super Bowl victory.

Prelude

Magic was in the air; faith was contagious; and maybe God had a plan for New Orleans after all. The city, having soldiered through the horrors of broken levees and floodwalls, had reached the pearly gates. The immaculate grail, the Vince Lombardi Trophy, was within its grasp.

Who dat? Who dat? Who dat say dey gonna beat dem Saints?

The signature chant of the Who Dat Nation resounded like a fervent tribal war cry. The greeting "Who dat, baby" rolled off tongues with all the familiarity of "Where y'at, dawlin?" Christmas trees festively adorned with Saints regalia were still sparkling in February. Saints-inspired banners, flags and handcrafted signs were everywhere—usurping the usual seasonal decorative blitz featuring the colors of Mardi Gras Madness: purple, green and gold. Black and gold had become the ubiquitous representation of an entirely new, although related, phenomenon: Super Bowl Party Gras Madness.

In an interview with MardiGrasUnmasked.com a few days before the Saints delivered the ultimate blessing in Miami, Amy Kirk, marketing director of the historic New Orleans French Market, likened the pre-Super Bowl atmosphere to Mardi Gras 2006. Back then, it was like a homecoming for locals; people came together in the streets for an emotional outpouring of communal solidarity, sharing their love for New Orleans.

Now everyone was smiling through their tears over the heroic glory march of the Saints. Kirk said she didn't realize how caught up in the fervor she'd become until hearing a pop Who Dat song on the radio. The tune was "very girly, for lack of a better description, but it totally made me cry. I was like, 'What is going on?' " (Later, she was amused to learn that the song was a Saints remix of Miley Cyrus' *Party in the U.S.A.*)

Powerful forces were, no doubt, coalescing in the Crescent City. Garrett Hartley's game-winning field goal in overtime against the Minnesota Vikings in the NFC Championship game had unleashed a tsunami of euphoria that would crest two weeks later, on Super Bowl Sunday (Feb. 7), and keep right on rippin' and rollin' through Fat Tuesday (Feb. 16).

Eight days before the date with destiny in Miami, Carnival revelry kicked into high gear with the Krewe du Vieux parade. Harking back to early incarnations of pre-Lenten festivities, when buffoons and rabble took to the streets to make merry and mock the elites, the notoriously iconoclastic and wacky procession evokes do-it-yourself performance art, with homemade costumes and mule-drawn floats.

For the 2010 parade, each of seventeen "sub-krewes" presented a unique take on the theme "Fired Up!" Flaming innuendos directed at politicians mixed with joyful illumination of the city's all-consuming, fired-up frenzy over the Super Bowl-bound Saints. One unit in the parade, the Krewe of PAN, committed to a Saints "sub-theme," "VOODAT," even before the team had clinched a berth in the Super Bowl.

The krewe decided that celebrating the Saints was so important that it would

break from its tradition of presenting racy satire and, instead, spread the gospel of New Orleans voodoo magic. In its interpretation, a mysterious priestess conjured incantations hexing opposing teams and love potions for rapturous fans of the home team. No wonder the Colts were doomed.

Who Dat hysteria had already reached a fever pitch in the local media when a rallying call went out to the Who Dat Nation: ABC's *Good Morning America* was coming to town for a live "Super Bowl Block Party" broadcast from historic Jackson Square on the Friday before the Big Game. Fans were urged to turn out in force at 5:45 a.m. to represent for the Black & Gold.

Anchored on the scene by Robin Roberts, a native of Pass Christian, Miss., who had reported extensively on the aftermath of the flood, the program was a picturesque postcard of New Orleans and Saints spirit—featuring a second line led by Troy "Trombone Shorty" Andrews and Kermit Ruffins, plus appearances by Mardi Gras Indians, celebrity Super Fans, even dogs dressed as Who Dats. Chefs from local restaurants in the Emeril Lagasse empire whipped up Super Bowl fare including Who Dat Hot Crab Dip (cream cheese, mayonnaise, onion, garlic, sautéed bell peppers and Louisiana blue crab meat).

Roberts told viewers: "It seems like everybody's saying 'Who Dat' all across the country. They don't know what it means, but they're saying it." Not even locals could agree on the origins, evolution and meaning of the phrase. But as John Romano of the St. Petersburg *Times* affirmed, "Who Dat" spoke to the "devotion" and "irreverence" of Saints fans, and to "the spirit of a city that refused to stay down."

On Super Bowl Sunday, that spirit took the form of a giant "pup rally" otherwise known as the Mystic Krewe of Barkus parade. Having begun as a quaint French Quarter promenade with a few dozen costumed party pooches, Barkus is now a popular Mardi Gras extravaganza with elaborate floats, thematically attired human escorts and a royal court with preening dukes and duchesses.

The idea for the canine masquerade was hatched upstairs at Good Friends Bar in the French Quarter in 1992, at a meeting of an informal fan club of WDSU-TV Meteorologist Margaret Orr. Thomas Wood's dog Jo Jo was present at the gathering. As legend has it, Wood decided to create a Mardi Gras krewe for his pup to lord over, as Queen Barkus I and then "captain-for-life," as a way to get back at friends who had dared to call attention to her neurotic ways.

Alas, doggie heaven beckoned before Jo Jo could live the dream of seeing the Saints in the Super Bowl. With the team just hours away from taking the field in Miami, the atmosphere along the parade route was abuzz with excitement and anticipation. Tails of black-and-gold doggies wagged wildly at the thought of feasting on the meaty bones of roasted Colts.

Chew Dat!

On the day before the Super Bowl, a Who Dat hanky giveaway and second line culminated in a prayer ceremony at the statue of St. Joan of Arc. She is known as the Maid of Orleans for heroically leading the French army in a rousing victory against the English in 1429, lifting the siege of the French town of Orleans. The banner she had made to carry into battle was emblazoned with fleur-de-lis. (A heraldic emblem of French kings, the stylized representation of a lily or iris flower was destined to become the symbol of New Orleans and its NFL franchise.) The unofficial patron saint of the Crescent City, she was canonized in 1920. Invoking St. Joan as an "instrument of righteousness" and "divine justice," the faithful prayed for her to intercede on behalf of the New Orleans Saints, "to grant us this final victory."

Signs and offerings left at the base of the statue, on the eve of a momentous battle.

St. Joan's statue is located near the French Market, the scene of the Who Dat hanky rally. A Saints flag hung over the statue's banner for two months, before and after the Super Bowl. Orchestrating the flag raising and hanky rally: the French Market's Amy Kirk, who is also founder of the Krewe de Jeanne d'Arc, which parades on the pious peasant-girl-turned-warrior's birthday, on Twelfth Night (January 6).

The Krewe of PAN's "VOODAT" presentation caused a sensation at the Krewe du Vieux parade. A New Orleans voodoo priestess transformed krewe members into life-size voodoo dolls representing all the teams the Saints had whipped. The float memorialized the victims with fanciful tombstones.

A participant in the sub-krewe Rue Bourbon, doing her part to stoke Who Dat hoopla.

As part of its "Farewell Roast" of outgoing Mayor Ray Nagin, another unit of the Krewe du Vieux, the Krewe of C.R.U.D.E., served up Cochon de Ray (a play on Cajun roast pig, otherwise known as Cochon de lait), specially prepared by renowned chef "Paul Prudpig." The flying pig is apropos of the Saints having clinched their first-ever Super Bowl berth.

When ABC's *Good Morning America* came to New Orleans in search of over-the-top fanfare for its Super Bowl Block Party, which aired live on the Friday before Super Bowl Sunday, Who Dat central casting didn't disappoint. Iconic musicians Kermit Ruffins and Trombone Shorty threw down with celebrity Super Fans in full regalia. They were joined by revelers in love with a team whose winning ways had become a catalyst for optimism and civic engagement.

Both Kermit and Shorty hail from the historic Tremé neighborhood and, fittingly, play themselves in the HBO series of the same name. Focusing on musicians and culture-bearers who struggle to retain their folkways and rebuild their lives after the city flooded, *Treme,* which debuted in April 2010, has introduced a large audience to Mardi Gras Indians and other indigenous customs that most tourists never get to experience.

Back in the summer of 2009, Kermit, a fanatical Saints fan, recorded a Christmas album for Basin

Feeling the spirit with Supa Saint, Whistle Monsta, Gris Gris Man, Fleur-D-Licious, Voodoo Man and Randy Elvis. In a city where eccentricity is a civic virtue, indulging alter egos through costuming is a way of life.

Street Records that included the single "A Saints Christmas," with the line "All I want for Christmas is the Saints in the Super Bowl." By the time the album came out, he'd gotten an enormous fleur-de-lis tattoo inked across his chest. "I'm killing 'em when I take off my shirt at the beach," he told Wright Thompson of ESPN.com, for a story published before the playoffs. "Especially at the Super Bowl."

For the "Domecoming" in 2006—the first home Saints game at the Superdome after the hurricane—Trombone Shorty joined U2 and Green Day for a performance that packed an epic emotional punch (during the rousing anthem "The Saints are Coming," he got a shout-out from Bono). For the Super Bowl victory celebration parade (Lombardi Gras), the multi-talented "supafunkrock" phenom played with his band Orleans Avenue as honored guests on Saints owner Tom Benson's float. By April, when Verve Forecast released his major-label debut, *Backatown*, to wide acclaim, he was well on his way to breakout stardom on the national level.

Need Saints fans to turn out in force and get their groove on before sunrise? No problem.

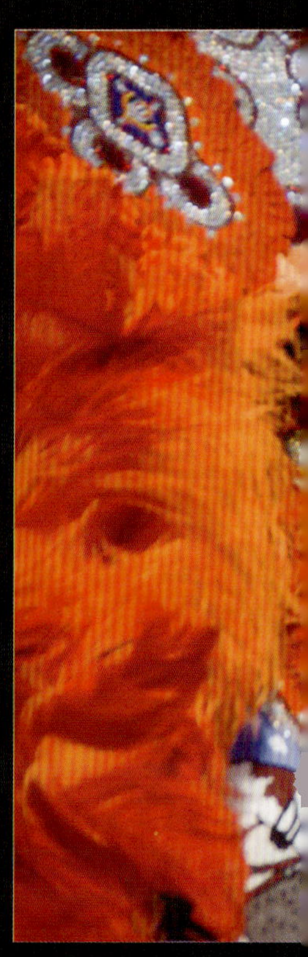

A Super Bowl rally with a New Orleans twist: Mardi Gras Indians, a brass band second line and gonzo fans that love to "represent." As they say down yonder in the Land of Dreams, "Dat's how we do, y'all!"

This talented Who Dat Dog, sporting his road jersey, shows he's ready for action in the Big Game.

A larger-than-life symbol of the city, Big Easy Dog went through hell yet managed to bounce back and enjoy life. Pet rescuers from Nebraska—who found him outside of the Superdome after the hurricane, starving and half alive—named him Big Easy Dog.

After a stint in Nebraska, he wound up at Orange County German Shepherd Rescue, in southern California, and underwent extensive medical treatment

Roberta LaGrand, a Shepherd lover living in Las Vegas, followed his progress via the Internet. After efforts to find his pre-Katrina family proved unsuccessful, LeGrand and her husband, David, adopted Big Easy Dog (bottom right). Apropos of his rescue, as well as the fact that he was born wearing black and gold and loves to watch Saints games on television, they nicknamed him "Dome Dog."

Before moving to New Orleans in the fall of 2009, the LeGrands ordered a commemorative bead in Big Easy's honor (above), to give away at the 2010 Barkus parade. His compelling story of overcoming adversity earned him a coveted position as a Barkus duke.

"I keep telling people that was the best day of my life: My dog was on the Barkus court, and my Saints won the Super Bowl," says Roberta. "It just doesn't get any better than that!"

In front of the St. Louis Cathedral, Sister Who and Sister Dat preside over a Super Bowl Sunday invocation.

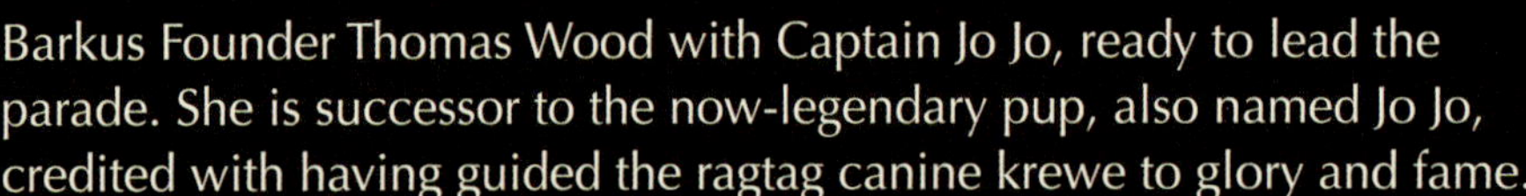
Barkus Founder Thomas Wood with Captain Jo Jo, ready to lead the parade. She is successor to the now-legendary pup, also named Jo Jo, credited with having guided the ragtag canine krewe to glory and fame.

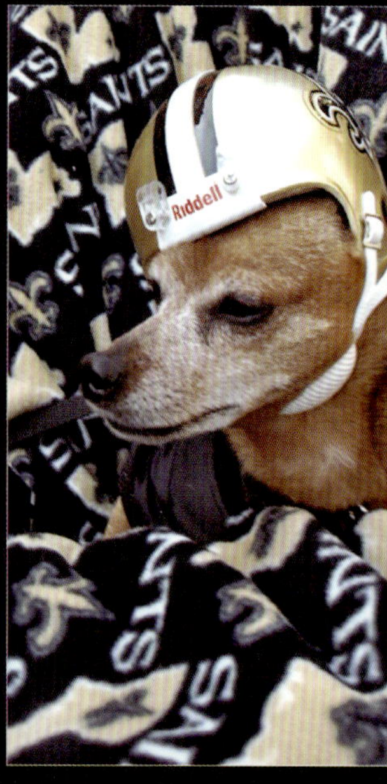

Like Bacchus and other Carnival krewes, Barkus has its own royalty. The queen is traditionally a Cinderella story—an animal-shelter mutt who has undergone a successful adoption—while her consort belongs to someone who has demonstrated a high level of commitment to the krewe. The 2010 king, Barkus XVIII, was Margaret Orr's dog Blue (left). The idea for Barkus originated at a meeting of the local meteorologist's "fan club," in 1992.

If human superkrewes can benefit from celebrity associations, why not the mystic canine krewe? Joining in the cavalcade as grand marshal was best-selling author, "pet lifestyle expert" and animal-rescue advocate Wendy Diamond (right), accompanied by her Maltese, Lucky, who was adopted from a New York City shelter in 1999.

The Treme Brass Band rolled with the parade (theme: "Barkus Goes Tailgating: The Dogs Go Barking In"). The salute to the Saints brought forth black-and-gold floats, feathers and frou-frou, plus a bone-anza of gridiron pooch puns. Some dogs dressed as their favorite players, like "Wide Retriever Barques 'Bigsby' Colston" and "Drew Fleas and the Flea Flickers." All present were feasting on the tastiest tailgate treat imaginable: the Saints in the Super Bowl.

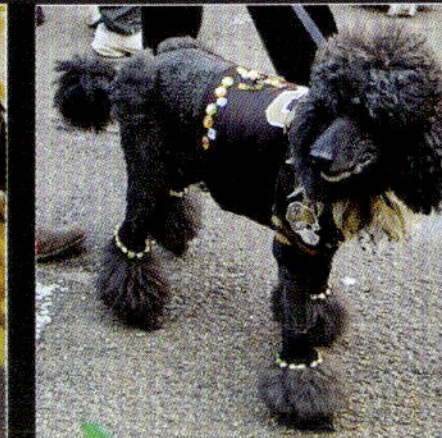

SAINTS

Barkus is known for having a strong family orientation. Thinking thematically, dressing up and decorating make for a fun and creative learning experience. And what's not to like about putting on a crowd-pleasing show?

Well-socialized dogs love attention, and Barkus is the ultimate attention-getter. Sometimes it seems as if the dogs are smiling, literally—like they "get it," understanding that the parade is all for them. The people are very happy and excited, too, and the dogs feed off that.

Idolization of the Saints by rabid human fans easily rubs off on their four-legged friends, who just can't stand being left out of the fun. This yellow Labrador Retriever dressed as one of the team's most popular and enigmatic players, tight end Jeremy Shockey, complete with stringy blond hair and tattoos running down his legs below the No. 88 jersey.

SAINTS

CRAW DAT

NEW ORLEANS

CBD
Parking
$20

THIS DRESS IS
FOR YOU
BUDDY

GEAUX SAINTS

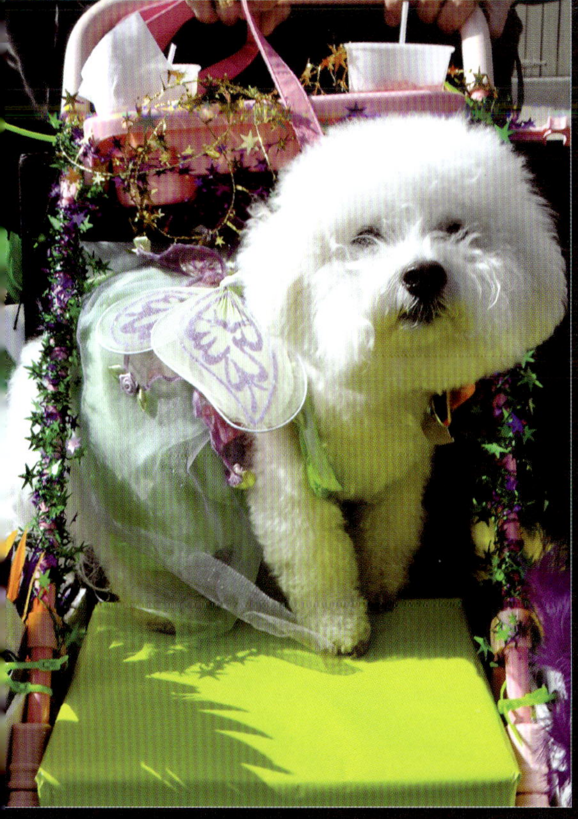

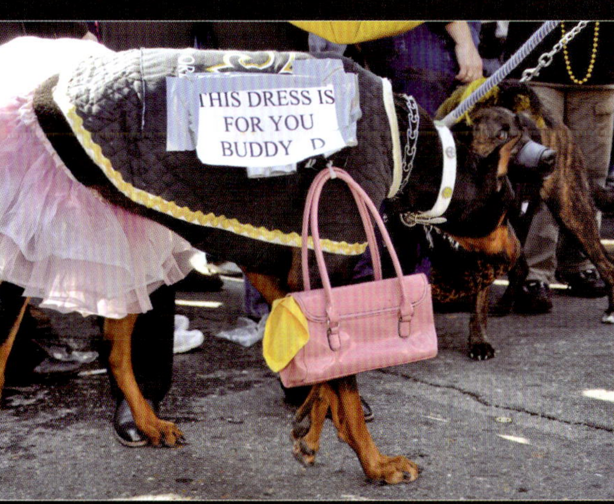

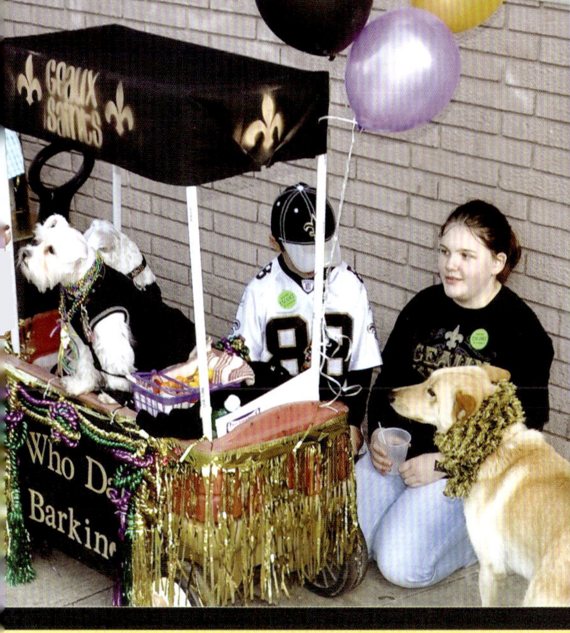

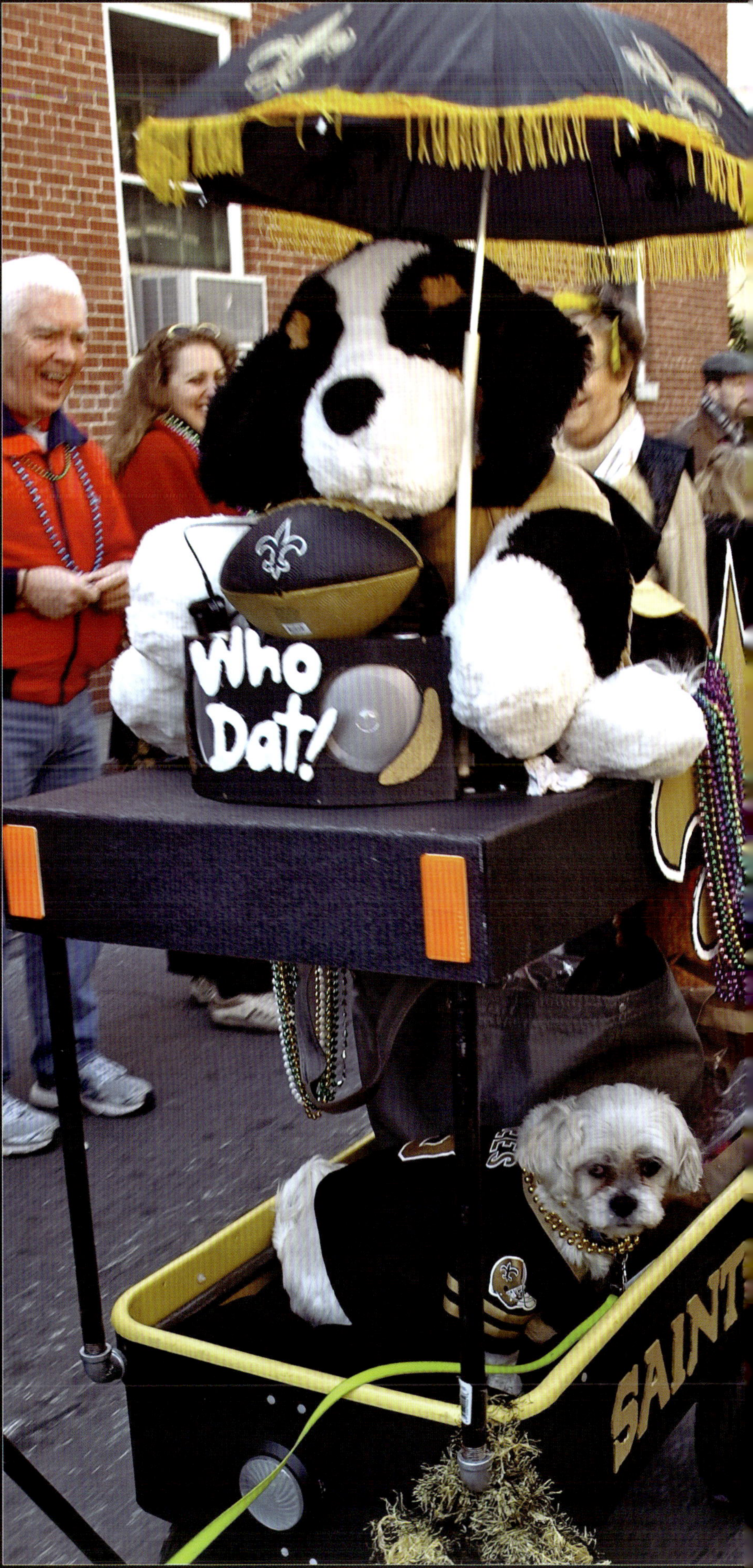
Who Dat!

Buddy D Gras

31 January 2010

What was supposed to be a fun little parade turned into a spectacular showing of solidarity and Who Dat couture. Thousands of joyful spectators turned out to salute "Buddy's Broads" as they marched from the Superdome to the French Quarter.

If there was ever a proxy for the hopes and frustrations of Saints fans, it was none other than Bernard Saverio Diliberto, affectionately known as Buddy D. Over a 50-year-plus career as a sportswriter and broadcaster, he became a beloved cult icon—"the sports heartbeat of the city," as his friend, former *Times-Picayune* columnist Angus Lind, once wrote.

Famous for mangled pronunciations, barbed commentaries and banter with fans calling into his talk show on WWL Radio, Buddy D was as passionate about the Saints as he was exasperated by their foibles and inadequacies. He once said, "When you go to Heaven after you die, tell St. Peter you're a Saints fan. He'll say, 'C'mon in, I don't care what else you done, you suffered enough.' "

On his radio show, when half-cocked callers would get excited about the possibility of the Saints making the

The happiest haloed Who Dat in heaven, Buddy Diliberto was surely smiling down on the dress-parade tribute and the torrent of creative energy it brought forth in his honor. Behold this beautifully crafted gold armoire shrine memorializing the late sports radio host and his famous Super Bowl dress pledge.

playoffs, and maybe even somehow punching a ticket to the Big Dance, Buddy D would laugh at their naiveté—only a "squirrel" could believe in such a thing. He vowed that if the Saints ever made it to the Super Bowl, he'd make a spectacle of himself by parading down the street in a dress.

Fans despaired of ever seeing the dress dream come true—the idea became a long-running joke—and Buddy D passed away suddenly in January 2005. Five years later, after the unthinkable happened—hell froze over when the Saints defeated the Minnesota Vikings and set their sights on Super Bowl XLIV in Miami—Buddy D's former colleagues at WWL came up the idea of a men-in-drag tribute parade. What better way to honor the "ultimate Saints fan" and his famous dress pledge?

Announced just a few days prior, the folks at WWL thought it would be a fun little parade. But it turned into a wild-and-crazy happening.

Leading the way was Buddy D's successor at WWL, former Saints quarterback Bobby Hebert, who'd made a few Super Bowl dress promises of his own. Now here he was fetchingly got up in a gold sequined mini-length muumuu and flouncy black slip, pleated and trimmed with lace. His blonde wig had Swiss braids and pigtails, topped off with a tiny tiara.

WWL News Director David Cohen reported live from the parade route. "A lot of people told us, as we were passing by: 'This is the best parade ever. *Best parade ever.*' I asked, 'Better than a superkrewe during Mardi Gras?' And they said, 'Oh, it's just so emotional, because it's all the Who Dats together showing such unity.' "

"If this is any bit of a taste of what it's going to be next Sunday when the Saints *win* the Super Bowl," Cohen noted, "*ho-ly cow.*"

The sparkling ladies of the Red Hat Society have nothing on festively festooned Who Dat fashionistas. From mini skirts and sundresses to formal gowns; from Heidi dresses and cheerleader outfits to strapless taffeta; from faux cheetah to delicate chiffon and vintage lace — virtually every fashion style was represented in homage to Buddy D.

The revelry, Hebert told sportswriter Hank Gola of the New York *Daily News*, "would eclipse anything this city's ever seen." Mardi Gras would turn into "a month-long party," he added. "Lent isn't going to slow it down. Who Dat Nation would say, 'No, God understands the circumstances. We didn't think this would happen.' "

Bourbon Street was packed for the dress parade, though not with tourists. One caller to WWL dubbed the occasion "Buddy D Gras." Hebert, who broadcast live from the Oceana Grill after the parade, responded by saying, "Let me tell you right now: I'm rolling down [the street] in the parade, and no matter where we turned the sun was shining on the Who Dat Nation. I was looking up at the sun and saying, 'Thank God for the New Orleans Saints.' "

"Nowhere in America this happens. Nowhere!" Hebert declared.

Indeed. A police car leading a parade of men in drag (with beers in hand and rolling coolers full of more cold ones) as they strutted and shimmied through the Central Business District, hamming it up for onlookers every step of the way—with cigars, decorated parasols, hairy legs and all.

We Made It
HEAVEN
SENT

For Bobby Hebert, being a member of the Who Dat Nation is not so much a fan identity as it is a lifestyle—a consuming passion that expresses New Orleans' renowned culture of revelry, theatricality and masquerade. He should know. From his perch as sports talker on WWL Radio, the former Saints quarterback and native of Lafourche Parish, in Louisiana's Cajun country, popularized the term "Who Dat Nation," and is often referred to as the tribe's founding father. Flamboyant, outspoken and unabashedly demonstrative, he exemplifies its exuberant, extroverted spirit.

Hebert's daughter, Cammy Lynn, who resides in Manhattan, created his dress especially for the parade. It so happened that she was launching a new fashion line called Show Me Your Mumu, in partnership with designer and style commentator Cologne Schmidt. In an interview with Hank Gola of the *Daily News*, she described the flashy one for her dad as the "Mu Dat Nation Mumu." She was hoping he'd wear fishnet leggings. "That would really complete the look," she told Gola. Alas, dad opted for a black-and-gold garter.

Mack the Quack (left) was among the celebrity Super Fans who joined Hebert for the joyride. WWL colleague Deke Bellavia suited up in Hebert's old Saints uniform. They shared the limelight with legions of other costumed crazies who, collectively, personified Super Fandom, Who Dat-style.

The Cajun Cannon

For some Who Dat dames, squirrel fur was to die for.

As these signs implicitly acknowledge, Buddy D spoke for an amorphous segment of the local population that has become identified with the term "Yat," which is derived from the colloquialism "Where y'at?" (translation: "How are you doing?" or "Hello"). Yat "culture" is characterized by a strong affinity for customs, predilections and linguistic mannerisms that are particular to New Orleans and its surrounding parishes. "Gawd" is an example of Yat dialect.

Mardi Gras came early to New Orleans when the Saints made it to the Super Bowl and legions of Who Dats in drag took to the street with beers in hand. "Bless Ya Beer" echoes a popular expression referencing Saints players: "Bless You Boys."

On Buddy D Gras, the outpouring of affection for the late king of local sports radio merged with the collective euphoria over the success of the Super Bowl-bound Saints.

For New Orleanians raised on Mardi Gras merriment and make-believe, costuming is not only a form of creative self-expression but a way of life. In the Buddy D parade, young Who Dats readily joined in the cross-dressing. It was one of life's most unforget-table father-son moments.

There were, unquestionably, plenty of nutty goings-on at the Buddy D parade. Do one's eyes deceive, or is this granny really wearing a hat with a photo of a squirrel drinking from a can of Budweiser with a straw, under the inscription "I Believe"?

The frumpy granny look, to be sure, had a lot going for it—not just as a practical accommodation to beer-bellied physiques, but also as a way to indulge accessory fetishes.

Canonization was long overdue for Buddy Diliberto, who covered the Saints from the team's inception and, despite enduring decades of ignominies on the field, remained a steadfast diehard—the "ultimate Saints fan."

Buddy D was never afraid to use his media pulpit to speak unvarnished truths, even if it meant upsetting Saints management, so one can only imagine the wry denunciations the NFL Who Dat controversy would have elicited from him. The NFL had paid scant attention to Who Dat, a catchphrase in the signature cheer of Saints fans. But after the team punched its ticket to the Super Bowl and Who Dat exploded into the national consciousness, the league clumsily tried to elbow its way into the driver's seat of the merchandising bandwagon by issuing cease-and-desist letters to mom-and-pop T-shirt shops, citing trademark infringement. Which made for an enticing, if unintended, story line: Folks who had lost practically everything a few years earlier to floodwaters were now at risk of having Who Dat taken away by a bullying "No Fun League." Louisiana politicians eagerly joined in the ensuing furor—championing the cause of the Who Dats and threatening the NFL. With media outlets stoking the uproar, the league defensively claimed there was a "misunderstanding," and that it had only meant to discourage the use of Who Dat in combination with "official" logos and trademarks.

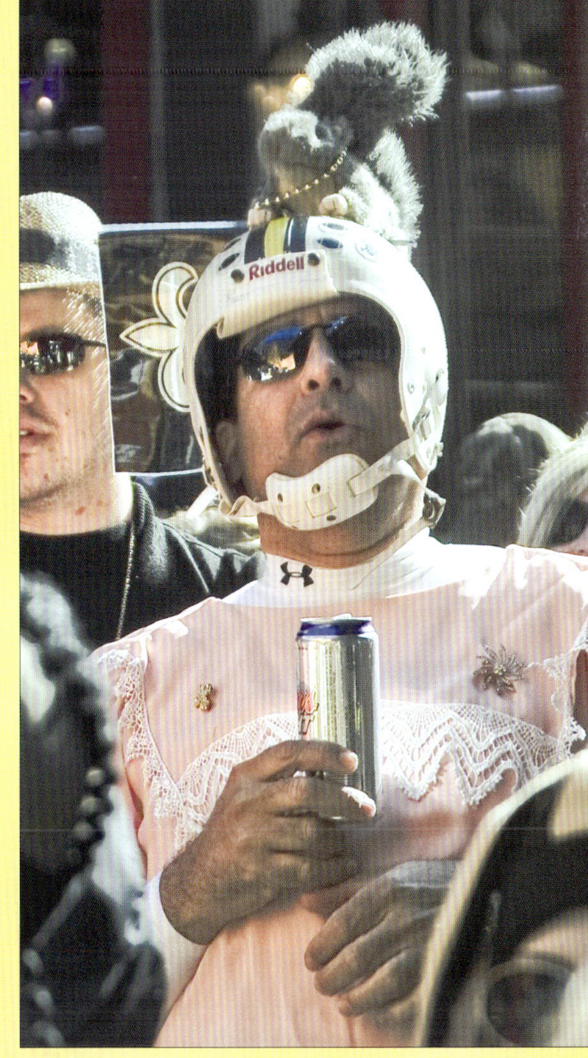

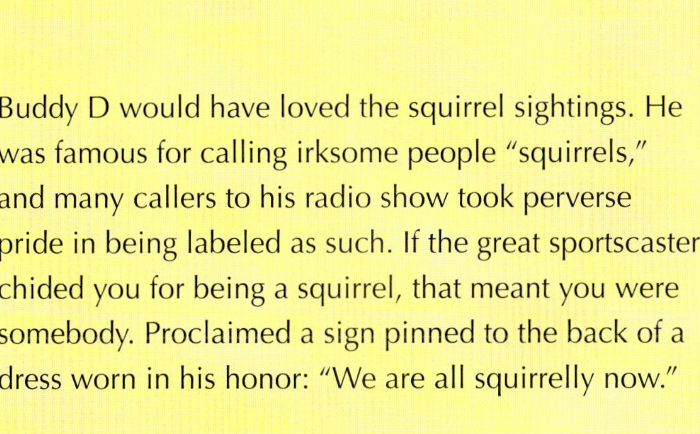

Buddy D would have loved the squirrel sightings. He was famous for calling irksome people "squirrels," and many callers to his radio show took perverse pride in being labeled as such. If the great sportscaster chided you for being a squirrel, that meant you were somebody. Proclaimed a sign pinned to the back of a dress worn in his honor: "We are all squirrelly now."

Although the sainted Diliberto passed on before he could make good on his promise to don a dress if the Saints made it to the Big Dance, his legacy was such that even the most manly of men felt compelled to represent for him—and perhaps strike a saucy pose or two for good measure.

For the crafty ladies and gents of the Who Dat Nation, the fashion accessory du jour is a decorated umbrella. By the time the dress parade rolled, fleur-de-lis trimmings were in short supply. Like a drum major's shiny baton, the umbrellas are both ornamental and functional. In the moving celebration dance known as the second line, revelers spin and pump them in rousing expressions of New Orleans-style joie de vivre.

Even Shetland ponies wore their best black-and-gold dresses. Dey all axed for you!

Ooh la la, madame–who dat say chic décolleté?

Hey, doll, f'sure beginning' to look a lot like Mardi Gras!

In the realm of regalia, festive adornment and bling bling, the Who Dat Nation simply refuses to be outdone.

The parade ended up at Oceana Grill, site of a massive block party and "Best Dress" and "Hairy Legs" contests.

Simply getting to play in a Super Bowl was enough to attract flying pigs to the French Quarter.

Amidst all the hoopla, the faithful found ways to memorialize brethren who, like Buddy D, didn't live to see the Saints make it to the Super Bowl. Was this black-and-gold coffin doing double duty as a beer cooler? If so, an all-the-more fitting tribute to dearly departed Who Dats.

Prancin' and dancin' and gettin' dat crunk on, y'all. For some famously animated Saints fans, making a spectacle of oneself can almost be second nature.

Buddy's Broads Gone Wild: cheap thrills from naughty "girls" on Bourbon Street. Live and uncensored!

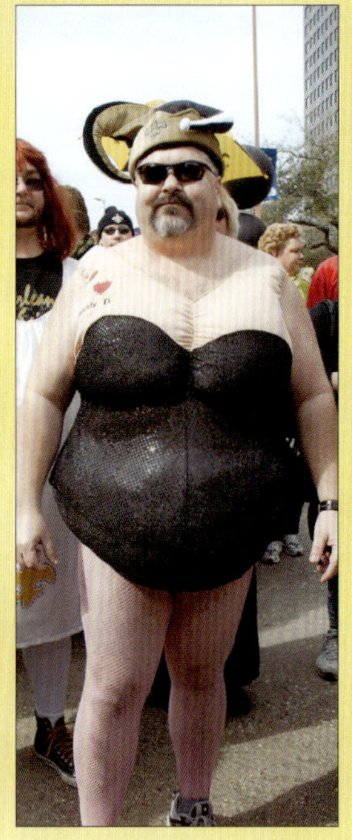

In dat number, baby–and ready for my closeup.

With a fabulous pair of shades and a Zulu afro wig, a ho-hum ensemble is transformed into something Saint-sational.

Games
Bourbon
Foot Locker

SAINTS

RETIRED
THIS IS PAYTON DURING THE SUPERBOWL
THIS IS PAYTON AFTER SUPERBOWL
WHO DA
BIGGEST
BROAD
BIG JOHN
FROM MID-CITY

Lombardi Gras

9 February 2010

What other city with a team going to the Super Bowl would announce plans before the game for a celebration parade, *win or lose*? CBS *Late Show* host David Letterman, who had Drew Brees as a guest the night after the Super Bowl, was impressed. "Isn't that great?" he asked.

Brees: "That's one of the things you love about New Orleans—we know how to throw a party, and doggone it, any excuse to do it, we're gonna do it. But I'm glad we won so we can make it even better."

The next night—exactly one week before Fat Tuesday—New Orleans experienced "Lombardi Gras" (or, as Saints play-by-play announcer Jim Henderson dubbed it, "Dat Tuesday"). The over-the-top extravaganza featured razzle-dazzle Mardi Gras floats conveying Saints players, coaches, cheerleaders, staff and family members.

Drawing a crowd variously estimated at 500,000 to 800,000, the parade generated unprecedented levels of excitement and traffic gridlock, and left commentators grasping for superlatives. It was, by some accounts, simply the "best parade ever."

In the dens of Kern Studios, the folks responsible for building almost all of the big Mardi Gras parades had labored under tight deadlines to pull together a doozy. Coordinated by Barry Kern, CEO and son of Kern Studios founder Blaine Kern, aka Mr. Mardi Gras, a plan took shape calling for various Carnival krewes to lend signature floats for the celebration parade.

An all-star lineup was quickly assembled, along with marching bands and dance troupes. Never before had the likes of the Rex *Jester* float, Zulu *Warrior* float, Orpheus *Smokey Mary*, Muses *Shoe*, Alla *Allagator* and Tucks *Jolly Roger* been seen together in the same cavalcade.

But if Lombardi Gras would follow the format of a Mardi Gras parade, the usual dynamic—of everyone having their own little parade party and getting caught up in the mania for catching throws—simply didn't apply. An entirely different set of expectations was in play. For spectators, it was more about giving—expressing thanks to the team for bringing the joy of a championship to New Orleans—than receiving or merely being entertained. The throws tossed by the players were almost superfluous. What mattered was catching a glimpse of the heroes and bearing witness to history.

Spontaneous Who Dat chants and thunderous, cheering ovations erupted. When the parade paused, spectators swarmed around the floats to get autographs; the players were more than happy to oblige. Rolling along, they leaned over to high-five fans.

It's one thing to see players having fun celebrating a play on the field. But at Lombardi Gras, they were like exuberant kids on the loose—bounding around, dancing on the floats, even jumping off to make merry in the streets.

Quarterbacks and the offensive line on the Bacchus king float. The visually stunning Lombardi Gras production set an almost impossibly high bar for any other city hosting a championship parade.

They led chants, offered toasts and tributes, and sang along to (what else?) the ubiquitous anthem of the Saints' season: "Halftime (Stand Up and Get Crunk)" by Atlanta rap duo the Ying Yang Twins. (The floats were rigged with microphones and powerful P.A. systems.)

The scene at Gallier Hall was dramatic. Confetti rained down through bright beams cast by giant spotlights crisscrossing the cold night sky, evoking Academy Awards-style fanfare. Brightly illuminated Saints and Super Bowl logos were projected onto the façade of the iconic Greek Revival building.

Sean Payton rode on the last float, the massive *Smokey Mary* choo-choo train. Having slept with the Lombardi Trophy, aka "Tiffany," on the night of the Super Bowl, the victorious coach now kissed it repeatedly, blew kisses to the crowd and triumphantly held it aloft for all to admire, rapturously. At Gallier Hall, where politicians and dignitaries gathered, the *Smokey Mary* stopped for a toast.

"Here's to the best Mardi Gras week in the history of this city," Payton proclaimed.

For coach Sean Payton, the sterling silver football wasn't a fancy ornament to be polished and locked away in some corporate boardroom. It was, rather, a communal talisman to be rubbed and kissed and hugged. In one surreal moment during the parade, pandemonium ensued when he got off the float to let the faithful touch the trophy.

Saints owner Tom Benson with wife Gayle (above). A native son (St. Aloysius, class of '44), he shouted "Who Dat" into a microphone from atop the Endymion grand marshal float. Heroine granddaughter Rita Benson LeBlanc (left), executive vice president of the Saints, also rode. The float featured a giant replica of the Lombardi Trophy and gold fleur-de-lis animated with fiber-optic lights.

Saints executive vice president/general manager Mickey Loomis gave Payton his first head coaching job. Also instrumental in hiring Drew Brees, he has a nose for diamonds in the rough.

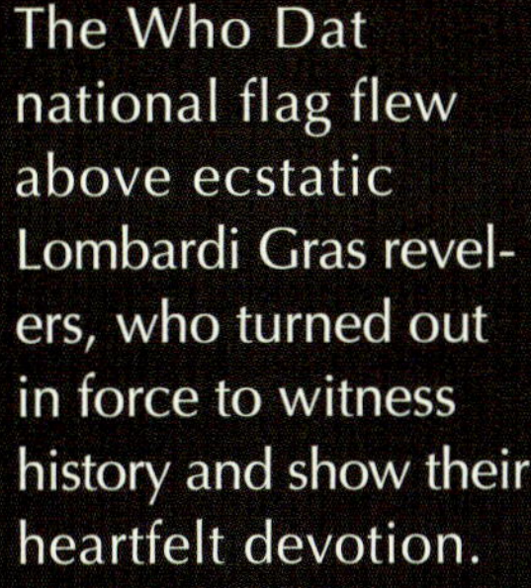

The Who Dat national flag flew above ecstatic Lombardi Gras revelers, who turned out in force to witness history and show their heartfelt devotion.

Deese boots were made for celebrating Dem Boys.

Images of joyous fanfare from the Lombardi Gras parade were seen by hundreds of millions of people around the world.

The players were as excited to party with the fans as the fans were to party with them. With his sparkling eyes and pageboy cap, Saint Drew—the new favorite son of the Crescent City—radiated youthful exuberance, whooping it up with the crowd.

Although Mardi Gras maestro Blaine Kern (left) has been bringing big-name entertainers to New Orleans to ride in parades for over 40 years, you never see him climb atop celebrity floats to pose for paparazzi shots. Lombardi Gras was an exception, he said later, describing Brees as "a sweetheart."

McDonogh 35 flag girl performing for the biggest crowd to ever watch a parade in New Orleans.

Frigid temperatures were hardly a deterrent for revelers intent on feeling the love. By some estimates, upwards of 800,000 spectators—roughly twice the population of New Orleans—were on hand for the gala.

Running back Pierre Thomas on the Krewe of Caesar officers' float. From undrafted free agent to heroic champion, on top of the world.

While Lombardi Gras had the trappings of a Mardi Gras parade—high school marching bands, glitzy floats and outstretched hands grabbing for throws—it was of a different order of magnitude. New Orleans put its best foot forward and showed the world it could represent in a style all its own. No overturned cars, broken windows or bad craziness. Just unbridled elation, gratitude and razzamatazz.

Instantly identifiable in their white Super Bowl jerseys, running back Reggie Bush (above) and his teammates had a ball simultaneously acknowledging and stoking the excitement and euphoria exuded by hundreds of thousands of highly emotional fans.

Most of the players had never ridden in a New Orleans parade.

It didn't seem to matter that Endymion-caliber showers of big beads weren't in the offing at Lombardi Gras. The atmosphere was so crunk that the energy level just fed off itself, generating plenty of gleeful interaction between players and fans.

SUPER BOWL
XLIV
Champions

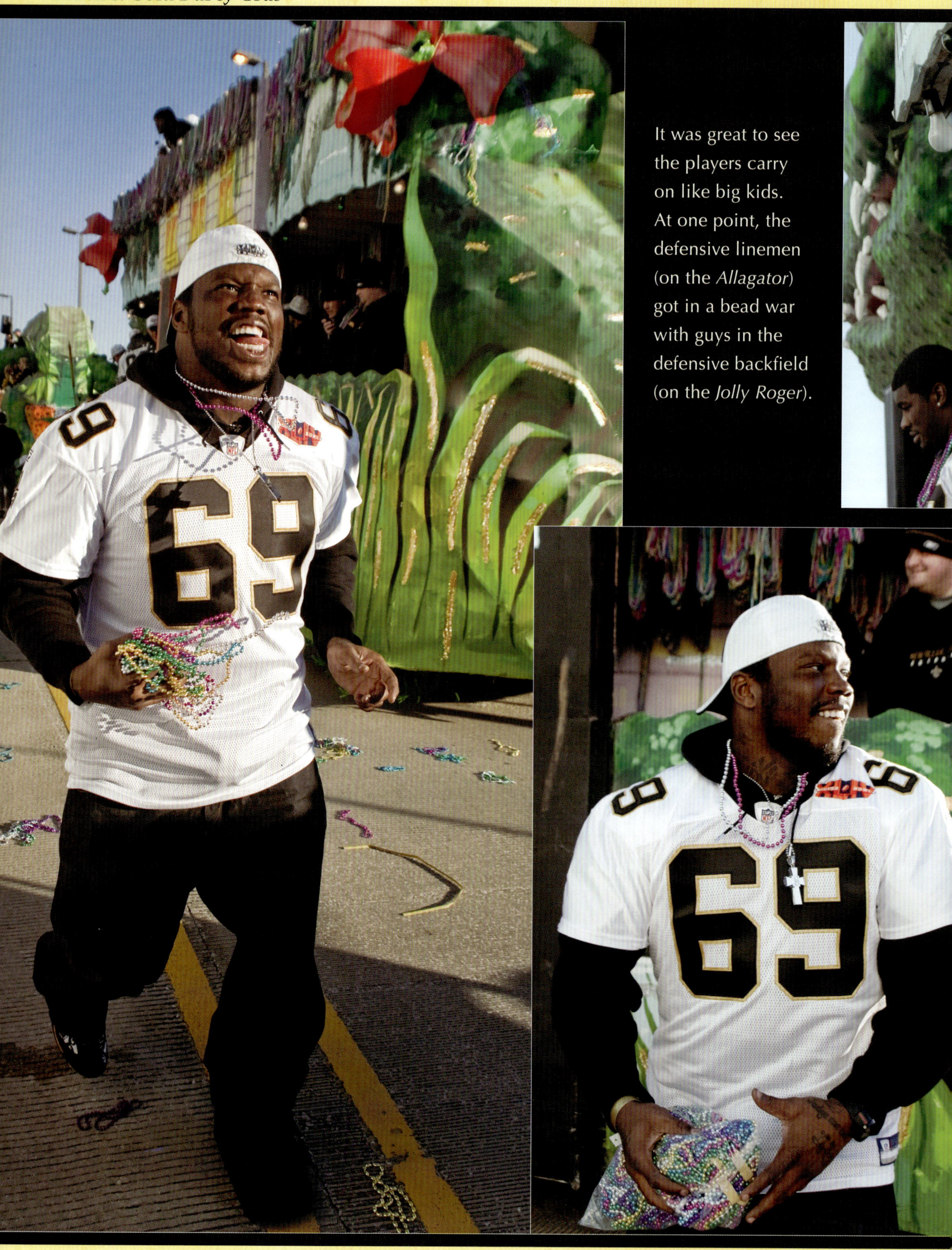

It was great to see the players carry on like big kids. At one point, the defensive linemen (on the *Allagator*) got in a bead war with guys in the defensive backfield (on the *Jolly Roger*).

Enjoying the action in the staging area alongside the Superdome. Maybe the best part about Lombardi Gras was seeing the players have so much fun.

Not all fans that managed to get near the floats were seeking autographs; some created commemorative keepsakes to give to the players.

The view from the floats must have been awe-inspiring, with revved-up black-and-gold revelers packed deep along the entire route.

During the season, the defensive backfield, led by safety Darren Sharper (#42), had consistently stolen the football away from opposing offenses. Their booty-reaping ways inspired Saints play-by-play man Jim Henderson to coin the moniker "The Pirates on Poydras." So how appropriate to see them on a pirate ship float, having the time of their lives rolling down Poydras Street from the Superdome en route to Mardi Gras World, just upriver from the convention center.

In an on-the-scene interview with ESPN's Rachel Nichols, Sharper was clearly fired up about the celebration. "We ain't stopped," he declared, "and we're not gonna stop.

"Dem boys!" he hollered, pumping his fist in the air. "Dem boys!

"Yeah, that's what we're doin', uh-huh."

The players had no use for the safety straps that usually tether riders securely to their berths on Mardi Gras floats. They climbed the rigging of the pirate ship and sprawled themselves along on its rails; danced and sang; and leaned over to high-five enraptured fans.

Sharper explained to ESPN's Nichols the modus operandi of Lombardi Gras. "We're mixing Mardi Gras and Super Bowl together. We're bringing it all together," he said. "Because that's what we did as a team: we brought it all together."

Sometimes it was hard to tell who was having more fun—the players or the fans.

On the *Jolly Roger*, as reported by Paula Devlin of Nola.com, Darren Sharper, Tracy Porter (#22, below) and Usama Young (#28, right) belted out the anthem "Halftime (Stand Up and Get Crunk)" with such fervor and "were rocking out so hard that at one point the float itself literally rocked…."

A parade party for the ages, Lombardi Gras was the ultimate expression of team spirit.

Fans came out early, dressed warmly and didn't hold back.

Brother Martin Crusader mascot with a black-and-gold Lombardi. Homemade Lombardi trophies would become popular accoutrements for Who Dat Party Gras happenings leading up to and including Fat Tuesday.

The Saintsations rode on the Zulu *Warrior* float, braving the cold with bare arms for the greater glory of the Who Dat Nation.

In the staging area, ready to roll with adrenaline still pumping from the Saints' electrifying Super Bowl victory.

With their black-and-gold finery and stylin' dance moves, the Saintsations would be an outstanding addition to the Zulu parade.

They seemingly came out of nowhere. "Ordinary men with extraordinary moves" and shiny gold shoes, the 610 Stompers—so named because the group's founder holds season tickets in Superdome section 610—caused such a sensation in the Buddy D parade that they got the nod to show off their choreographed, disco-era moves in the main event.

Dr. Martin Luther King Jr. Charter School band. In parade appearances, all the marching bands seemed to be playing the "Get Crunk" theme song of Black and Gold Party Gras.

The ceremonial head-dresses, or miters, of these holy Who Dats proclaim, "Bless You Boys." The popular saying goes way back, having appeared on signs at the old Tulane Stadium. With a catchy song for a series of Saints promotional spots, WWL-TV turned it into a mantra.

O. Perry Walker High School marching band at Gallier Hall.

Long snapper Jason Kyle (top), punter Thomas Morstead (left) and place-kicker Garrett Hartley. They came through in the clutch, and Lombardi spectators got a big kick out of seeing them ride in a shoe float.

The heartthrob hero saw many signs of love.

Hartley was on Canal Street when, in his midst, the Walter L. Cohen High School marching band came to a standstill. Caught up in the spirit of the moment, he borrowed a pair of pom poms from a cheerleader and launched into a spontaneous routine.

Hartley hopped off the *Shoe* float to fraternize with enthralled fans lining the barricades. The young Saint couldn't resist reciprocating the outpouring of love and devotion.

The famously flamboyant Who Dat Nation was uniquely well equipped to celebrate the historic moment. Because when it comes to partying and dancing, Saints fans are truly in a class by themselves.

Having endured the nightmare, it was time to live the dream.

Gallier Hall—the old city hall designed by renown New Orleans architect James Gallier and dedicated in 1853—provided a majestic backdrop for toasts and shout-outs from longtime Saints public-address announcer Jerry Romig and other notables.

Krewe Dat Nation

With the swaggering Saints bringing the Lombardi Trophy home to parade through the streets, just as the festivity of Carnival was nearing its Fat Tuesday peak, New Orleans had become the center of the universe. Announced Jason Gay in the *Wall Street Journal*: "Mardi Gras is now a permanent state, and you're all expected on Bourbon Street within the next seventy two hours, or you're fired."

On that infamous thoroughfare, the value of flashy fleur-de-lis beads as a trading commodity had hit and all-time high, and revelers were aglitter at the prospect of every parade becoming an extended black-and-gold Who Dat party for the city and the Saints.

After the extraordinary emotional high of the Super Bowl and Lombardi Gras, Mardi Gras was the frosting on the victory cake. The heroism of the Saints ratcheted up the anticipation factor and made people look forward to the seasonal rituals in a way they could only previously have dreamed about.

On one level, Mardi Gras was the perfect excuse to extend the Super Bowl celebration into a New Orleans-style party marathon. But it also presented the perfect forum for the city's endlessly inventive citizens to do what they do better than anyone else: take a theme and run with it.

The theme would translate on many levels, above all else making Mardi Gras 2010 probably the most festive ever. More men in dresses carrying on in honor of Buddy D. Marquee Saints players on floats in superkrewe parades. Spontaneous get-crunk dances on the route. Saints signs, banners and regalia everywhere. An incredible array of costumes saluting the team. Bright sunshine with warming temperatures going into the final weekend and prevailing straight through Fat Tuesday. The King of New Orleans, Drew Brees, as Bacchus. Zulu Who Dat coconuts.

And that incredible trophy, that shining symbol of triumph over adversity, being presented to the faithful. "Everybody that's here to-night can't touch this," coach Payton said upon reaching Gallier Hall in the Lombardi Gras parade. "And I know on behalf of the team and the organization, we just wish you could spend one night with it. Because your support and just your following means so much to us."

Now here he was in the Orpheus parade on the eve of Fat Tuesday, coming down off his high rolling throne to walk the walk among the Who Dats on Canal Street. And not just for a token minute or two. Back and forth across the street he went, for at least 15 minutes, beaming a huge grin and holding forth the sacred object for all to touch.

No, it simply couldn't get any better—or any more real—than this.

Brees and his wife, Brittany, avidly invested themselves in the civic and philanthropic life of the community. For Bacchus, they rode in the cockpit of a magnificent chariot float specially built for the occasion, bedazzling multitudes.

The stock-in-trade of the highly irreverent and entertaining Krewe d'Etat is topical satire. Tiger Woods, former Congressman (and convicted felon) Bill Jefferson, Ponzi schemer Bernard Madoff, New Orleans Mayor Ray Nagin and others were royally roasted in accordance with the theme "d'Etat's Inferno: A Not-So-Divine Comedy." A counterpoint to all the hellfire was a float entitled "Paradiso," offering a fanciful interpretation of hell freezing over in the wake of a Saints Super Bowl victory piloted by a winsome "Cool Brees."

As if to clearly demonstrate there are no "sacred cows," even Tom Benson and Rita Benson LeBlanc were in for a ribbing: a float depicted the Superdome, which is owned by the State of Louisiana, as their personal "Super Piggy" bank. Regardless, after the Super Bowl win, over joyed Saints fans weren't begrudging the team owner the opportunity to indulge in his signature celebration dance, the Benson Boogie.

On the Saturday before Mardi Gras, magic was definitely in the air for the biggest parade of Carnival, Endymion. Theme: "Abracadabra."

As the 2010 Mardi Gras parade season drew near, Tom Benson let it be known through representatives that he wished to partake in the festivities. His quarterback had already accepted an invitation to reign as Bacchus, and his coach had agreed to ride in Orpheus as part of the krewe's contingent of "celebrity nobility." The Krewe of Endymion answered the call, announcing Benson as grand marshal of its extravagant procession. As his float turned off Carrollton Avenue and headed down Canal Street, he seemed like a man 50 years younger as he gleefully pumped the Lombardi Trophy in the air. At his side was his wife, Gayle.

Some observers suggested that after the intense exhilaration of the Super Bowl and Lombardi Gras, Mardi Gras would be anticlimactic. But it wound up being a sprawling stage for a citizenry eager to partake in a dramatic expression of civic pride. At Endymion, the Who Dat multitudes demonstrated why there ain't no party like a black-and-gold neutral ground party.

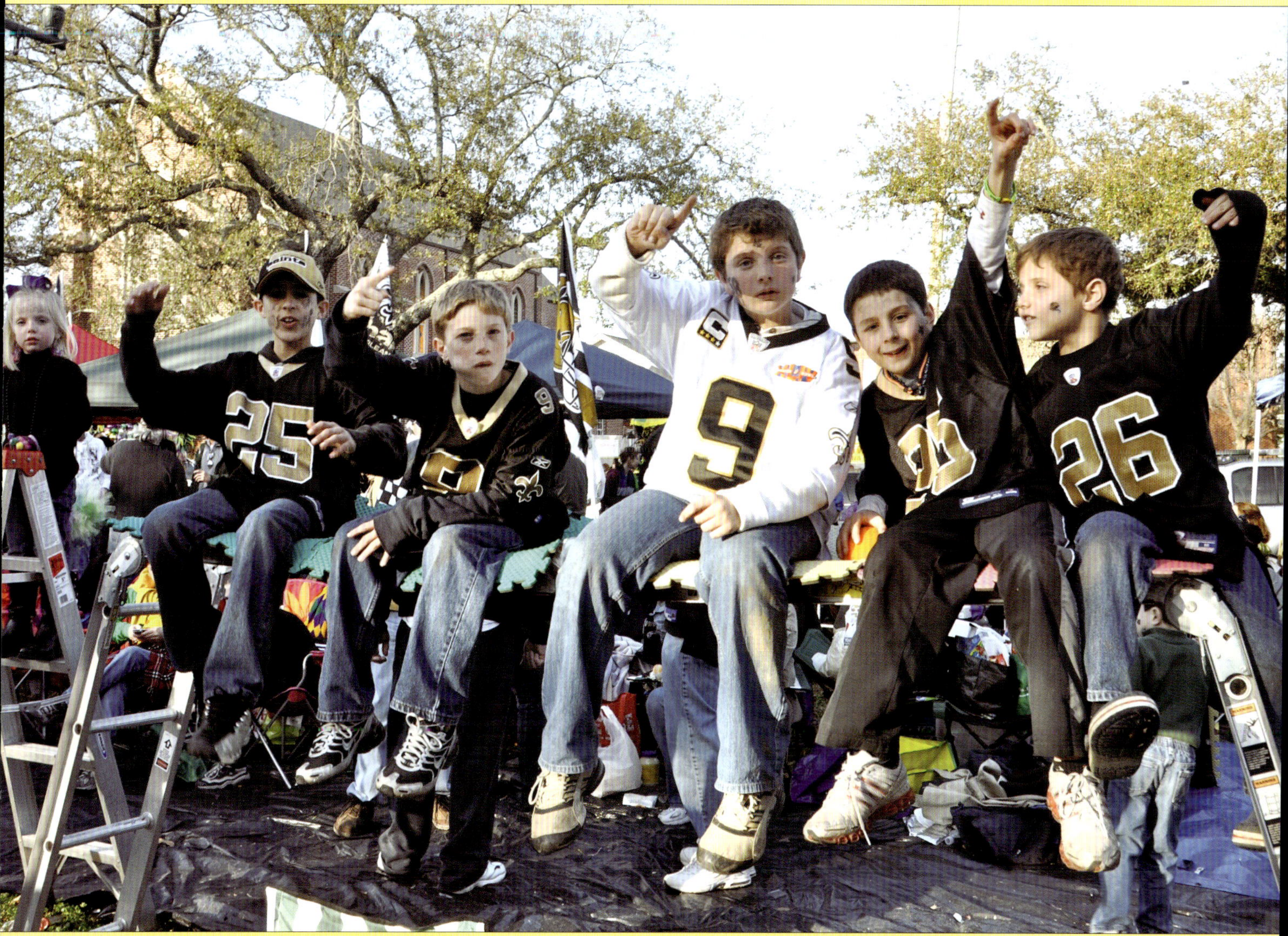
25
9
26

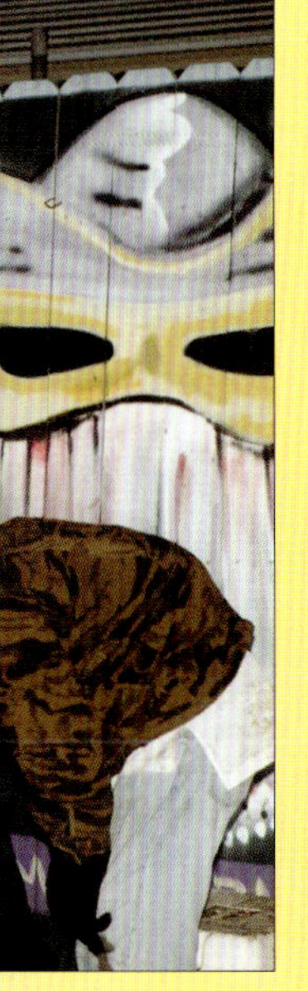

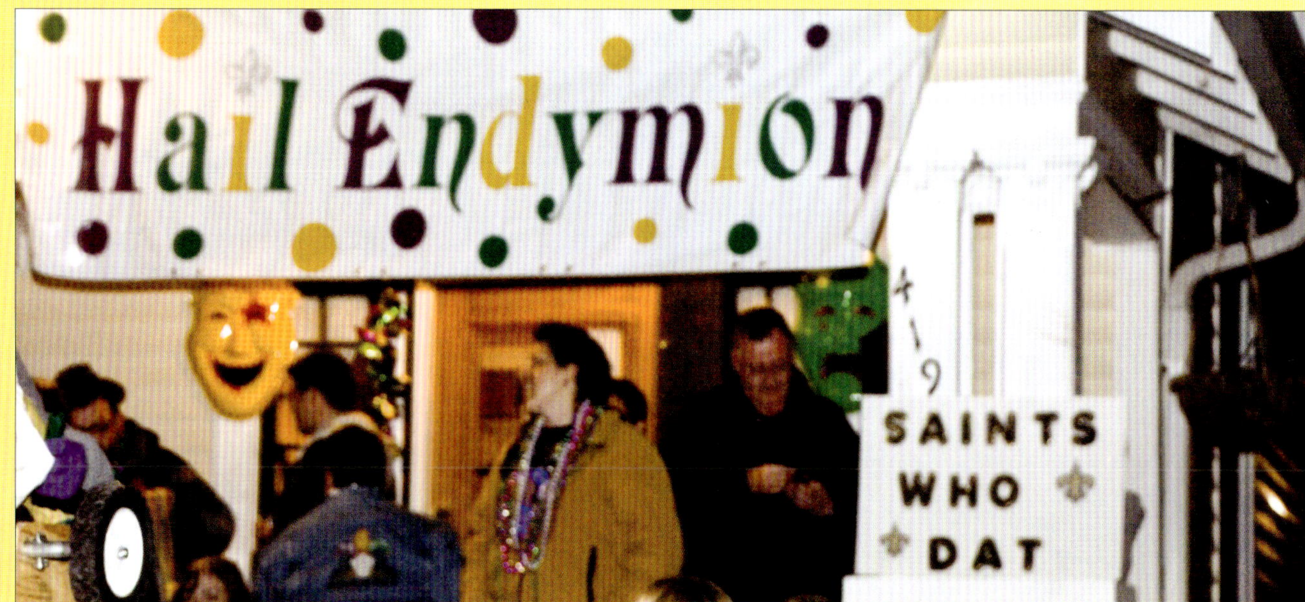

Hail Endymion
419
SAINTS
WHO
DAT

Before the parade, the Bensons and Saints kicker Garrett Hartley boogied on stage at the Endymion Samedi Gras Festival in Mid-City, as the Bucktown Allstars played "When Saints Go Marching In." Afterwards, in the parade staging area, fans mobbed Benson LeBlanc's float, whose riders included Hartley, linebacker Jonathan Vilma and defensive end Will Smith (above). The players happily obliged the autograph seekers, including one who handed up a replica of the Lombardi Trophy.

Wearing dark sunglasses, the heroine showed no sign of having taken stitches the night before, after getting hit in the eye with beads thrown at the Hermes parade. At one point, when the "Black & Gold (Who Dat!!)" version of "Halftime" began blaring from the float's P.A. system, she gamely raised her arms to rally the crowd to get crunk. Alongside the float, a fan held aloft a sign with just one word: RITA.

Saints symbols and Who Dat salutes were everywhere.

On Valentine's eve, feeling the love and jubilation.

SPS

Magic and sorcery through the ages was the subject of the 2010 Endymion parade, with some 2,400 float riders participating.

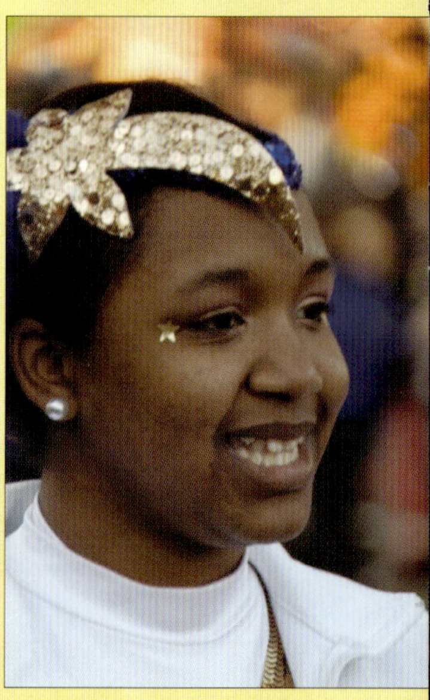

Revelers on a roll: An atmosphere of affirmation permeated the pageantry, with big smiles, tingles of anticipation and expressions of Who Dat pride lifting the spirits of a populace that had endured much frustration and hardship.

For throw-mongering compatriots of the Who Dat Nation, acquiring parade booty is a lively sport, with the winners taking home the biggest haul. Enticing targets help tilt the playing field.

Decorative and artistic Party Gras impulses were manifested in myriad ways.

Rolling with Box of Wine, a rambunctious bacchanal preceding the Bacchus parade. The headpiece depicts the Superdome inside a crescent, symbolic of the sharp bend where the Mississippi River wraps around New Orleans. The inverted crescent is a feature of the badge traditionally worn by the city's police superintendant.

Living large on the Bacchus title float. Rarely has such a generic Mardi Gras parade theme seemed so poignant.

The atmosphere on the parade route was hyperkinetic. One had the feeling that the assembled throngs would give just about anything to catch a blessed souvenir football from the man some called Breesus.

All hail the most heroic—and beloved—Mardi Gras monarch ever! Having guided the Saints to a fairy-tale realm overflowing with milk and honey, while also serving as a key catalyst in helping New Orleans recover from a deluge of mythic proportions, Brees, as Bacchus XLII, now reigned over a love fest for the ages.

At the urging of the mayor, even those without glasses had to mime a toast to the adored Party Gras Kingpin on this Valentine's Day.

Baccha
Berry
white

Wine and festive mirth, traditionally associated with the Roman god Bacchus, are elements of the *Bacchatality* float (left) ridden by krewe members who work in the New Orleans hospitality industry.

A flambeau amidst the fanfare at Gallier Hall.

On Canal Street, the crowd erupted when the parade stopped for Brees to receive a toast from Payton. The coach raised his glass of champagne from the balcony of the Astor Crowne Plaza Hotel, site of the Krewe of the Orpheus Captain's Party.

Payton and his wife, Beth. The victorious coach was a highly enthusiastic participant in Party Gras festivities.

A paparazzi moment on the balcony as Payton hoisted the trophy while surrounded by the likes of singer Taylor Dayne, actor Steve Zahn, LSU baseball coach Paul Mainieri and members of the band the Imagination Movers. All would be riding in the Orpheus parade as celebrity nobility the following night.

Everyone present seemed so energized over the Saints, amping-up the vibe from the usual high levels experienced during a Mardi Gras superkrewe parade.

Harry Connick Jr., co-founder of the Krewe of Orpheus, was born six days before the Saints played their first game as a newly minted NFL franchise. He grew up going to games at the old Tulane Stadium, and has a black-and-gold trumpet that he likes to play when the team scores a touchdown. The day before Orpheus, he sang the national anthem at the Daytona 500 and, when asked by the Associated Press about the Saints' Super Bowl victory, said: "It's just the greatest feeling in the world. And especially for it to happen right now around Mardi Gras time, in my opinion, it's the greatest time in the history of our city, at least as long as I've been alive." On Orpheus Monday, he told Natasha Robin of Fox 8 TV: "I think it's going to be a great steppingstone for our city to really see some brighter days."

Displaced for four-and-a-half years after the flood, longtime flambeaux supervisor Clarence Holmes (above) was finally back in town.

Imagination Movers (from left to right) Scott Durbin, Dave Poche and Scott "Smitty" Smith. The group, which also includes Rich Collins, formed in New Orleans in 2003, buying their trademark blue jumpsuits at Brown's Uniforms on S. Galvez Street. They went from performing at local birthday parties to landing a show on the Disney Channel (now seen in some 55 countries) and winning an Emmy. They've performed on *Good Morning America* and at the White House. But what could possibly top the thrill of being in the thick of the Black and Gold Party Gras?

The memory of a legendary sportscaster loomed large at Mardi Gras 2010. But even parade goers who might not have been familiar with Buddy Diliberto's pledge to wear a dress if the Saints made it to the Super Bowl seemed to find the spectacle of men strutting and shimmying in womanly garb worthy of approbation.

Mitch Landrieu rode on an Orpheus celebrity float with singer Taylor Dayne. His landslide mayoral victory, on the day before the Super Bowl, amplified the pride and elation over the Saints and hopes for a rejuvenated city's bright new future. Running on a message of unity (motto: "One team. One fight. One voice. One city."), he became the first white mayor-elect since his father in 1979. He encouraged citizens to follow the example of the Saints and see themselves as a team focused on a great outcome. In his acceptance speech, he quoted a text message he'd just received from Rita Benson LeBlanc of the Saints: "The people of the city did their part; now it's time for us to do ours." Then Landrieu urged everyone to "get ready for the Saints to take it all the way!"

Paul Mainieri and his wife Karen, accompanied by a plush version of LSU mascot Mike the Tiger, were in fine form on a specially outfitted purple-and-gold float. He directed the 2009 Tigers to the College World Series title, posting a 56-17 overall record.

At a press conference before Orpheus rolled, Zahn related that he once rode in a 4th of July parade, in Hancock, Minnesota, with his family on the back of a hay wagon. It wasn't too exciting. "Everybody played cards," he recalled. Pausing for effect, he then deadpanned, in reference to the Orpheus parade: "This is better, right?"

Steve Zahn continued an Orpheus tradition of featuring musical talent combined with national celebrities. On the HBO series *Treme*, in many ways an homage to the musical culture of New Orleans, he plays aspiring songwriter and part-time community radio station deejay Davis McAlary—a character based in part on the real-life New Orleans music scenester Davis Rogan. Each year, the superkrewe—whose mythological namesake played a mean lyre—salutes a New Orleans musical legend (in 2010, Snooks Eaglin) with a commemorative doubloon.

Preserving local music culture while keeping kids off the streets, the nonprofit Roots of Music offers free academic tutoring, instruments and music education to low-income middle-school students. Its marching band has become a fixture of Mardi Gras parades.

This float was completely themed out à la Saints, from the mascot prop to the flags and the riders' black-and-gold costumes.

If pigs were flying in honor of the Saints, there was no bigger Who Dat ham than Bobby Hebert. The sports-talk kingpin and former Saints quarterback seemed determined to "bless" each and every bead he threw.

There was never anything the least bit forced about Sean Payton's wholehearted embrace of Party Gras. The trophy seemed to bring out his generosity of spirit, as he worked the crowd with abandon and reveled in the sense of community underlying the celebration.

No stranger to the limelight and the celebrity culture of Hollywood, Reggie Bush, sporting black diamond earrings, seemed positively in awe of the theatrics that unfolded around him during the extended victory party. "It's part of history," he told Natasha Robin of Fox 8 TV. The fact that the illustrious Lombardi Trophy was being toted around "like it's a gym bag" just made everything seem all the more surreal. "It's almost like you feel you're going to wake up and it was all a dream, you know?"

Bush appeared on *Live with Regis and Kelly* when the show visited New Orleans back in April. "This year is going to be a great year for the Saints," he predicted. "We're going to go to the Super Bowl; we're going to go all the way."

During the Orpheus parade, Payton showed the same daring and penchant for surprise that he did in opting for an onside kick to start the second half of the Super Bowl (which may go down in history as the greatest Super Bowl call ever, as the Saints recovered the ball and drove for a touchdown to take their first lead of the game). When the "How Sweet It Is" float hit Canal Street, he got off to merrily share the Vince Lombardi Trophy with frenzied fans lining the route. It was as if the rock star coach was making good on his pronouncement during the trophy presentation ceremony at Sun Life Stadium in Miami, after his team won the Super Bowl in stunning fashion: "Everybody back in New Orleans gets a piece of this trophy."

Parade goers could hardly believe their eyes. Here was the hero perhaps second in line to be canonized (after Brees) personally presenting them with the trophy. At least one excited lady fan returned the favor by planting a big kiss on his face.

LEMONADE

te's Foot.

PACKAGE

POLICE
GOLDEN WALL
CHINESE RESTAURANT
TURN

GNC
N.O.P.D.
DINING CAR

1993
ORPHEUS' SMOKEY MARY

WHO
DAT
NATION

SAINTS

WHO DAT

An incredible Saints season inspired many collectible keepsakes.
Jewelry by Jeanette Meyer of Gypsy Junk Jewelry
Who Dat tile by Mark Derby of Derby Pottery & Tile
World Champions ring (left) by Heather Macfarlane of Unique Products
Muses Who Dat shoe by Libby Black on loan from the N.T. Broussard collection

By virtue of its official (black-and-gold) color scheme, Zulu is like one big Saints fan club almost by default. But the affinity runs deeper. The Zulu Social Aid and Pleasure Club and "Who Dat" grew out of the same tradition: blackface minstrelsy and vaudeville. Members of an African American group called the Tramps took up an African theme after having seen a musical comedy performance in 1909 that included a skit about the legendary king of the African Zulus, Shaka. "Who Dat Say Chicken in Dis Crowd?" was the hit song from the 1898 musical variety show *Clorindy: The Origins of the Cakewalk*—a landmark in black entertainment, with songs sung by a full black chorus and roles performed by an all-black cast led by comedian Ernest Hogan. Today, the Who Dat Nation and Zulu are stylistically similar in their zany flamboyance and irreverent theatricality.

Who Dat coconuts and black-and-gold mega balls had everyone begging.

When the Zulus go marching to "the good jumping music of brass bands" (as Louis Armstrong wrote of the sounds he heard in the parade as a boy), it's a spectacle like no other. The euphoria surrounding this year's festivities put some extra swagger in everyone's step.

Many participants in the Zulu parade came up with fun ways to mask for the Who Dat Nation.

Zulu favors generic, catch-all themes and allows for plenty of individual creative expression in costuming, totems and coconuts. This year, inspired by the drama surrounding the Saints, the krewe had its "A" game going.

Great hands and leaping ability count for a lot in the NFL. Here, a future Marques Colston demonstrates that the same holds true when it comes to snagging Zulu coconuts.

Zulu coconuts are always highly sought after, in part because they're decorated by hand and come in a variety of fanciful styles. This year, black-and-gold, Who Dat and fleur-de-lis designs were much in vogue.

Having begun as a small, informal marching group called the Tramps—a raggedy lot who affected the manner of hobos—the Zulus have evolved into a costuming tour de force.

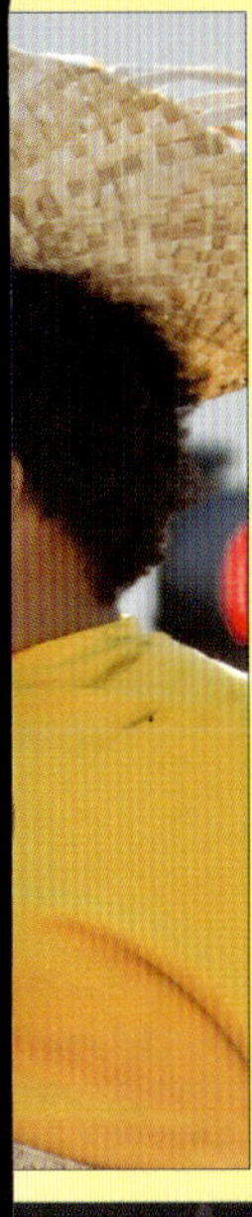

Limited edition 2010 Super Bowl coconuts caused a sensation.

Defensive end Charles Grant (left) made the most of his moment in the sun—rapping and dancing and raising a rumpus. Also riding: cornerback Randall Gay (below).

The contrast to the mayhem after the flood couldn't have been more striking. Canal Street was a scene of looting and desperation. Now came frivolity and catharsis, as the city of Mardi Gras merriment rejoiced in a fairy-tale dream come true.

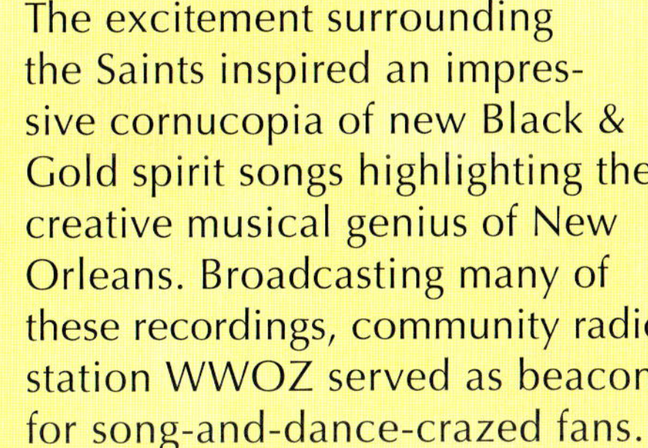

The excitement surrounding the Saints inspired an impressive cornucopia of new Black & Gold spirit songs highlighting the creative musical genius of New Orleans. Broadcasting many of these recordings, community radio station WWOZ served as beacon for song-and-dance-crazed fans.

Throws always add to the participatory excitement of Carnival parades. Stoking the mania at Saints Party Gras: black-and-gold beads and necklaces adorned with fleur-de-lis; souvenir footballs tossed by players; and coconuts commemorating the champions.

A defining (and at times controversial) element of the Zulu masquerade, blackface came to be interpreted as a satire of white stereotypes of blacks. But when the first Zulus blacked up in the early 1900s, it was more a practical matter than a subversive statement. The early members were a downtrodden bunch who couldn't afford to buy masks. A five-cent tube of face paint did the trick.

Even those not in costume found ways to show their Who Dat pride.

Bikini underwear are a standard, if not always practical, throw that beg the question: Where are the ladies petit enough to wear these Mardi Gras thongs? This masker, in coming up with a deluxe version of Who Dat lingerie, obviously had plus-sized booty in mind.

Originally, the standard Zulu costume consisted of black-dyed turtle-neck, black tights and grass skirt. Later, Afro wigs and gold boots became popular accessories. Nowadays, elaborate headdresses and other fancy finery are part of the krewe's Afrocentric burlesque.

You never see a sign with a plug on the float of Rex, king of Carnival and a stickler for tradition. But this year, in honor of the hometown heroes, an exception had to be made.

Costumes

Theme-wise, a black-and-gold Mardi Gras was a given. Much of the fun would come from seeing the myriad ways in which revelers would creatively amplify and interpret all things Saints.

Orleanians were in their element, no question. For in the city of Mardi Gras merriment, the pool of talent engaged in the creation of wearable art is as deep and formidable as the wellspring of musical and culinary genius. Costuming is a consuming passion and a lifestyle—the ultimate expression of the collective mania known as Mardi Gras Madness.

The act of costuming is called "masking," regardless of whether an actual mask is worn. Masking makes possible an escape into a world of fantasy. Thus, the prim executive assistant at a buttoned-down law firm emerges on Fat Tuesday as a Who Dat burlesque dancer. The computer wiz dismissed as a "geek" by football jocks in high school? He's a giant replica of the Super Bowl trophy named after the legendary coach who was machismo personified—Vince Lombardi.

The Saints' rumble through the playoffs set off a feeding frenzy for black-and-gold paraphernalia: tutus, gloves, feather boas, headbands, flowers, top hats—you name it. A couple of days before the Super Bowl, Broadway Bound Costumes on Canal Street was completely sold out of fleur-de-lis appliqués and other essential trimmings. "We still have glitter left," said Sonny Borey, whose family owns the store, "but that's about it." At Miss Claudia's Vintage Clothing & Costumes in Uptown New Orleans, Proprietor Claudia Baumgarten described the black-and-gold rush as "insane." People planning their Mardi Gras regalia, she said, "want to be Saintsations or Saints players or a Saints fairy or Saints devil—any twist on Saints and the Super Bowl."

When an overarching theme emerges, as it did at Mardi Gras 2006 and Black and Gold Party Gras, a variety of recurring motifs or sub-themes also, inevitably, come to the fore. At the first Mardi Gras after the flood, political and bureaucratic incompetence, FEMA trailers, abandoned refrigerators and blue tarps (the ubiquitous material used to cover wind-damaged roofs) provided bountiful fodder for revelers. Four years later, there were flying pigs, Lombardi trophies, black and gold and the fleur-de-lis—the symbol of the Bourbon monarchy of France, the City of New Orleans and the World Champion Saints.

In the French Quarter on Mardi Gras, trophy replicas seemed to be everywhere. The Lombardi had come to symbolize not just a football dream come true, but also the triumph over all the hardship and frustration endured in the wake of broken levees.

Like that first Mardi Gras after the flood, Saints Party Gras had become an empowering forum for commemoration and catharsis. The former was bittersweet, the latter all sweetness.

For locals, it simply wasn't enough to see the blessed Lombardi Trophy paraded through the streets. It had to be transformed into an object of idolatry and ritual replication—and thereby appropriated into the cultural vernacular. Mardi Gras became the vehicle for its communal sanctification.

A Fat Tuesday tribute to Sean Payton and the Holy Grail he brought home to New Orleans. The coach slept with the trophy the night of the Super Bowl and on the plane ride back from Miami.

MOO
DAT!

OUI
DAT

BRUNO
N.F.L.
"WHO DAT"
POLICE

THE REAL
HOUSEWIVES
OF WHO DAT
NATION!

WHO DAT
NATION
OF
ISLAM

WHO DAT!!
18
18

AINTS
NO
MORE
DOLTS
Indi is in
desparate
ed of brown
per bags!
DOLTS
Indi is in
desparate
need of brown
paper bags!

SAINT

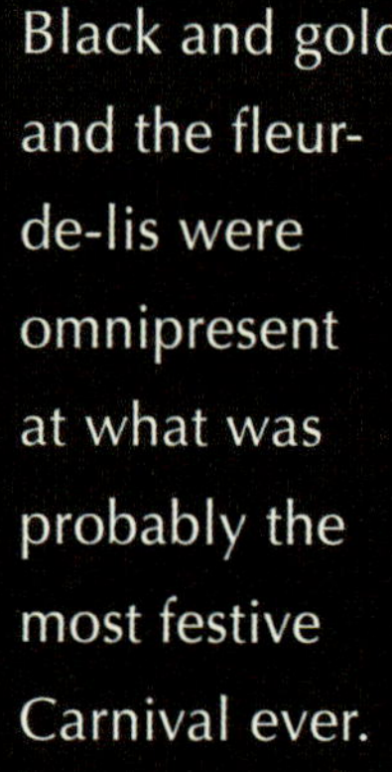

Black and gold and the fleur-de-lis were omnipresent at what was probably the most festive Carnival ever.

9

Diva
EST. 2002

BREES
9

pigs
fly

This duo (dig dem boots!) presented a superhero tribute to Saints wide receiver Marques Colston and cornerback Tracy Porter. "Mr. Significant" refers to Colston having almost been drafted as "Mr. Irrelevant"—the nickname given every year to the last pick in the NFL draft. (A seventh-round pick out of Hofstra in 2006—the 252nd pick overall—he holds the NFL record for most receptions in a player's first two seasons, with 168.) Porter had crucial 4th quarter interceptions in the NFC Championship and the Super Bowl.

Surely there could be no sweeter moment to memorialize than what took place on the field in Miami after the clock wound down on Super Bowl XLIV, when Drew and Brittany Brees celebrated with their one-year-old son Baylen. In this fanciful recreation, Baylen is sporting his "favorite toy" on his tiny wrist—a Lombardi Trophy rattle. "He was born here [in New Orleans]," said the proud mother, "and his first words were 'dat dat.' "

Signs of Affection

What is it about New Orleans that makes its citizens such prolific proponents of handcrafted signs?

Mardi Gras, no doubt, is a big part of it. It's a celebration of self-expression that invites everyone to become an artist. Playfulness and creativity shine in homemade decorations, props, costumes and signs.

When it comes to "throws"—beaded necklaces and other paraphernalia tossed to revelers from parade floats and balconies—everyone is looking for an edge. The thrill and challenge of acquiring the baubles becomes a competitive sport, summoning both animal urges and creative strategizing.

Float riders love to test their aim with throws, and parade goers with the most ingenious targets and signs make out like bandits. A popular variation at Saints Party Gras: designs challenging riders to show they could throw like Drew Brees, whose 71% completion rate in the 2009-2010 season set an NFL record.

Because New Orleans has so many parades, locals are especially well schooled in the art of party placards. Even refrigerators abandoned in the wake of the flood demonstrated a certain penchant for crafty linguistic shorthand. These so-called "Katrina refrigerators" containing rotted food became billboards for graffiti folk art, and some of the most widely noted inscriptions spoke to anxieties over whether the Saints would permanently relocate from New Orleans.

Fast forward to February 7, 2010. Moments after the dramatic Super Bowl triumph at Sun Life Field in Miami, during the CBS television broadcast of the Vince Lombardi Trophy presentation ceremony, a camera flashed to a sign in the crowd: "Canonize Brees Stat!" Two days later, the Lombardi Gras parade in New Orleans brought forth an incredible profusion of celebratory signage—thanking the team for bringing a championship to New Orleans, expressing love for individual players, and offering multiple permutations and interpretations of "Who Dat."

Signs with a Saints twist continued to pop up everywhere during Mardi Gras and beyond. Some proclaimed good riddance to the term "Aints," a derisive moniker associated with the losing ways of a bygone era. The infectious optimism surrounding the team and the city, meanwhile, found expression in a new catchphrase referencing the hope for back-to-back championships: "Two Dat!"

SAENGER
WE DAT!
WORLD CHAMPION
SAINTS

I ♥ #5
Garrett Hartley
We Love
Our Saints
#1 in our ♥s
#1 in the
nation!
Reggie's
DA
Fiya
LOVE
DAT
SHOCKEY
You make my ♥ MELT!
You
are "DA"
SH*T
#5
I ♥
Hartley!

WHO DAT?!
MARRY ME REGGIE!
#25
WE ARE IN A RELATIONSHIP
TRACY MF'N PORTER
I'LL HAVE YOUR BABY
DREW, WILL YOU BE MY VALENTINE?
ITS MY Birthday
DREWBILATION
EAUX SAINTS WHO DAT!!
THANKS TRACY PORTER!

WELCOME TO
BREES
CIRCLE

BREES
COULD
DO IT

WHO
Say They
Throw Like

Try to
BE
BREES
WHO
DAT
R U #9?

WE DAT

NEW
DAT
FROM
WISCONSIN
"FAVRE ON THE GROUND!"

THANK YOU

WE CAME FROM
CUCAMONGA
CA.
BE with OUR
SAINTS

Who
Saints

MEN
of da
WHO DAT
Nation
and Dere Mom-n-Dems
MEMBER LOCAL 43
"TEAMSTERS"

NEW ORLEANS
SAINTS
MY HEROES
MY
FUTURE

WHO
DAT
NOLA
DAT!

Geaux
Saints
TATTOO

Thank You
BOYS

Congrats
World
CHAMPS

OUR

HIT ME IF
YOU
BELIEVE
DAT!

WE ARE
New Orleans

SAINTS
SUPER BOWL
XLIV

Leonardo
TRATTORIA
558-8986
WHO DAT

BLESS-U-BOYS
U-DAT-AWSOME

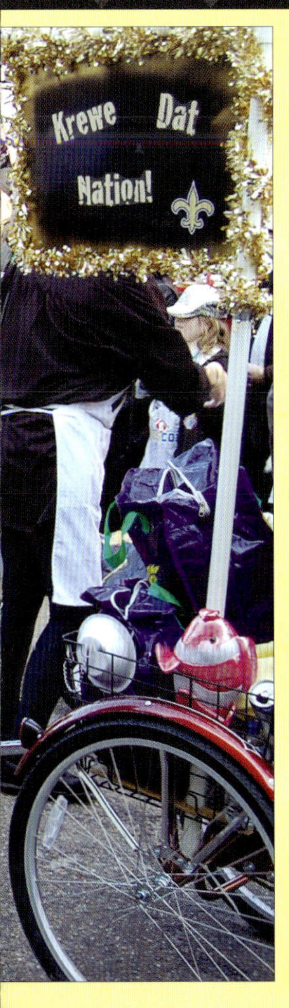
Krewe Dat
Nation!

WHO D@T!
SAINTS

Congratul
Saints Super Bow
XLIV

LOMBARDI
GRAS
VE OUR

our
Saints

GO SAINTS DRIVE
MIAMI BOUND
HOUND

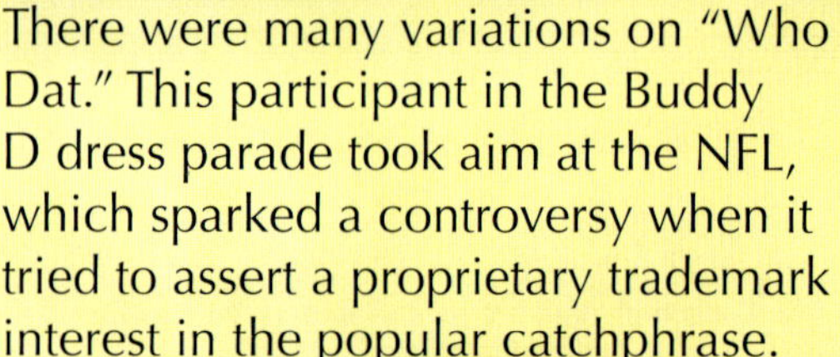
There were many variations on "Who Dat." This participant in the Buddy D dress parade took aim at the NFL, which sparked a controversy when it tried to assert a proprietary trademark interest in the popular catchphrase.

The shoe is the principal icon of the Krewe of Muses, and figures prominently in the all-female Carnival organization's arsenal of popular throws. Its most sought-after offerings are actual shoes individually decorated by krewe members. Such Mardi Gras "folk art" is highly collectible. These signs cleverly combine the Who Dat theme with the Muses shoe fetish. Float riders often reward such efforts with prized throws.

Aints Jazz Funeral

20 February 2010

Nineteen hundred and eighty. It was a year that will always live in infamy for older fans: the season of the "Aints." After having been in playoff contention in 1979, the hapless Saints started off 0 and 14.

Then sports anchor at WDSU-TV, Buddy Diliberto just couldn't take it anymore. Midway through the season, broadcasting before a Monday night game, he reached under his chair, grabbed a brown bag with "Aints" scrawled across the front and holes cut out for his eyes, and put it over his head. Inspired by the Unknown Comic of *The Gong Show* fame, he wanted to be an "unknown" Saints fan—anonymous in his ignominy.

Such antics come naturally to a citizenry steeped in the merry mockery of Mardi Gras. The Aints bags became a tradition—and a metaphor for futility—as fans took to wearing them at games. They were widely interpreted as a caustic statement about the Saints' humiliations on the field. But the real purpose arguably had more to do with fans' wanting to avoid embarrassment over their own inability to resist attending games, despite the likelihood of disappointment.

For this is New Orleans, a city that epitomizes diehard fandom and wrote the book on how to pass a good time following a mostly bad team. No fans have been more steadfast—as evidenced by the fact that, even before Drew Brees and Co. arrived on the scene, the Saints easily boasted the best average attendance per victory of any NFL club in history.

At the first Saints game, on September 17, 1967, New Orleans Archbishop Philip Hannan delivered a prayer before kickoff at the old Tulane Stadium. "Grant our fans perseverance in their devotion," he intoned. Thus began a journey not unlike that of the Israelites, who wandered in the wilderness for 40 years before finally entering the Promised Land.

When the ultimate redemption finally came, in Super Bowl XLIV, it was as if a hex had been lifted. Proudly proclaimed on signs seen throughout the Party Gras festivities, "Aints No Mo' " became a new mantra.

The Aints were done and gone, the brown bags relics of history, so what better way to mark their passing than to stage a New Orleans-style burial procession? It would be a jazz funeral unlike anything the city had ever seen.

A jazz funeral is an African American ritual in which

The Aints procession had all the trappings of a traditional New Orleans jazz funeral, including a grand marshal in ceremonial attire, brass band and horse-drawn hearse.

mourners and a traditional brass band escort the casket to the graveyard. It culminates in a party atmosphere, with a second line in which anyone can join in to celebrate the life of the deceased.

Mardi Gras was over, but here was a compelling excuse for one final, cathartic revel—a rollicking send-off for all things "Aints." Second liners came out in force, bringing with them Aints bags to place in a decorated casket—a symbolic repository for a legacy that had defined the Saints as loveable losers and perennial underdogs.

A few days prior, one of the organizers, Patrice Andrews Hall, penned an obituary for the infamous brown bag. "New Orleans Aints Paper Bag," she wrote, "born 1980, died February 7, 2010, was a resident of New Orleans for a short time. Survived by no immediate family, but a host of devoted fans."

The Aints casket is now part of the permanent collection at the Saints Hall of Fame Museum.

A highly theatrical affair, with a creative array of costumes and props, the Aints parade had a cast of colorful characters for which the Crescent City is justly famous. Here, a Native American Who Dat genuflected before papal impersonators, who offered a blessing in honor of our boys and the glory they bestowed.

Glenn Hall III (left), son of Patrice Andrews Hall and Glenn Hall Jr., plays trumpet for the Baby Boyz Brass Band. The band was joined by, among others, Glen David Andrews (right), cousin of Patrice. Along with the Halls, the acclaimed trombonist and showman organized the Aints second line.

The Aints affair, apart from being a fun roving party, expressed the multiculturalism of New Orleans. It was a fitting tribute to a team that unified the city across ethnic and class lines unlike anything previously experienced.

The Who Dat Nation takes great pride in elaborate homemade crafts and costumes. Above: Super Fan Whistle Monsta. Right: Impaled effigies of mascots representing the teams the Saints vanquished in the postseason.

Carrying a canvas-mounted photograph of a tomb marker bearing the inscription "The Aints, 1967-2010." *May they rest in peace* is superimposed.

SAINTS

I FEEL
YOUR AIN

AINT'S
AINT'S NO MORE

MID-CITY
CARRIAGES

BRASS

RIP
AINTS
AINTS

AINTS DERE
NO MO!
AINTS DERE
NO MORE

SAINTS
AIN
WORLD CHAMPIONS
AINT'S NO MORE
WE
DAT

The procession began in the Tremé neighborhood and ended on Frenchmen Street in Faubourg Marigny (above). It was the last big Party Gras event, although replica Lombardi trophies—along with Saints songs, second line umbrellas and jerseys—were common at the New Orleans Jazz & Heritage Festival, on consecutive weekends at the end of April and beginning of May.

The Party Gras Team

Black and Gold Party Gras manifested itself in many ways, and no single photographer could have captured the full scope of the delirium as it unfolded. Hence, this book is a collaboration almost by necessity.

All of us feel a compulsion to document what makes New Orleans special and share our love of the city and its beguiling idiosyncrasies with anyone willing to pay the slightest attention. Thank you, Saints, for having made possible this 100% positive representation of New Orleans.

Pat Jolly

Pat is effusive in discussing the Buddy D parade. "That was one of the most fun days of my life," she relates. The euphoric vibe emanating from the cross-dressers of the Who Dat Nation was so "contagious" that it "catapulted you into their revelry, and I wasn't expecting to fall into that. It was magical."

That's quite an endorsement. For few have immersed themselves more fully in the sensual cornucopia of the Crescent City than Pat Jolly. A tireless advocate for indigenous culture, she has made her mark as a photographer, arts educator, video producer and promoter of creative talent. She is also well known for her impish joie de vivre; and indeed, her nicknames—Jollyllama, the Funtrepreneur and the Night Mayor—testify to her determination to enjoy life to the fullest.

Over the years, Pat has been active in a variety of music-oriented community organizations and initiatives. During the 1980s, her passion for promoting music at the grass-roots level found an outlet in assembling a free day-by-day listing of local music gigs; printed weekly, it was popularly known as the Jolly Jazz Calendar. She has lent her listings expertise to magazines (*Wavelength, Where, Offbeat*) and community radio station WWOZ. Since 1993, she has spent countless hours keeping subscribers to her community e-mail service informed about performances and events, gatherings and fundraisers, art markets and exhibitions, funerals and celebrations, book signings, lost pets and much else.

Pat's most lasting legacy will be her voluminous photo collection. Her ultimate goal is to have it cataloged and organized into an online database that would serve as a resource for journalists, educators and anyone else interested in exploring the culture of New Orleans. It is a vast treasure trove in need of a preservationist patron (ideally, someone with a keen interest in New Orleans music).

"When it's all over," says Pat, "all you have are the photos and memories. But the photos help you keep the memories."

www.PatJolly.com
Pat@PatJolly.com

Kim Welsh

Kim is a psychologist, avid Saints fan and photographer with a passion for documenting musicians and cultural events including festivals, second lines, Mardi Gras Indians and masqueraders and jazz funerals. From the juke joints of the Delta to the backstreets of New Orleans, she enjoys people watching, all genres of music, ethnic cuisine, world travel, wildlife and children of all ages. An advocate for cultural preservation through respectful documentation, she uses visual imagery to encourage an understanding of unique world views and to remind people of how diverse performance traditions enrich our lives.

A native of Hattiesburg, Mississippi, Kim first started loving New Orleans as a wide-eyed kid, visiting Canal Street emporiums with her mother. In high school, Kim cut her teeth as a reveler at the Warehouse, the legendary all-ages, general-admission venue in a sketchy Uptown neighborhood on the banks of the Mississippi. From 1970 until it closed in 1982, it was *the* place to commune with legends such as the Allman Brothers, Bob Marley, Pink Floyd, Bob Dylan and Led Zeppelin.

Kim was chosen as a volunteer photographer for the 2010 New Orleans Jazz & Heritage Festival. She does event photography for The French Market Corporation and Young Leadership Council, and her work regularly appears in *Offbeat* magazine. A blues music aficionado and "fest junkie," she also writes for STLBlues.net and JamBandsOnline.com. If you happen across her vending at the Juke Joint Festival in Clarksdale, Mississippi, Crescent City Blues and BBQ Festival or Congo Rhythms Festival, be sure to check out her stunning images of New Orleans cultural events and bluesmen such as Little Freddie King, David "Honeyboy" Edwards and Pinetop Perkins.

www.Facebook.com/SlurpOysters
SlurpOysters@gmail.com

Lisa DuBois

A photo artist based in New York City, Lisa didn't know quite what to expect when she arrived at the staging area for the Bacchus parade, not long before a phalanx of policemen, with arms interlocked, escorted Drew Brees to his float amidst a frenzy of excitement.

For the most part indifferent to sports, she hadn't even watched the Super Bowl. Arriving in New Orleans for Mardi Gras, she had little inkling of the mania engulfing the city. Now, as the highly anticipated Bacchus parade began to roll, she found herself experiencing something extraordinary.

"The energy that I felt just permeated through my entire body," she recounts. "I felt like I had been there when the Saints won. I became one with the people and how they felt."

This "transference of energy," as Lisa calls it, is a facet of parades and festivals where participants have a message or reason to celebrate. "That's why I can be dead tired and still stay on my feet and photograph," she says.

Donning regalia for a parade or painting one's face on game day transports a subject into a zone where a different personality emerges. This transition from reality into the "fantasy moment" is what sparks Lisa's imagination. "In one 125th of a second," she says, "you can capture a moment that can create a tremendous multitude of emotions that last forever."

A graduate of the Germain School of Photography in New York City, Lisa is also drawn to the zone between fantasy and reality in her non-documentary work. Using computer software, she produces thought-provoking surreal images from her original photographs of the natural world. An interest in philosophy and metaphysics, as well as painting and design motifs found in nature, informs her artwork. She is certified as a hypnotherapist and tarot reader.

www.DuBoisPhotoArt.com
LisaDuBois@verizon.net

Mark Sottek

Along with his friends Karla Baker and Patti Hogan, Mark set out from Metairie for the Lombardi Gras parade, determined to snap a lot of pictures. "It was a parking lot in every direction," he recalls. "All the tricky ways of getting into the city were just as crowded as the major thoroughfares." Gridlocked on Earhart Expressway, they wound up parking the car and walking several miles to catch the parade at Gallier Hall.

A native of Laguna Beach, California, Mark settled in New Orleans in 1985. "I came for Mardi Gras," he says, "and decided this was the perfect place for someone as eccentric as me."

Mark brought his first computer in the early 90's, and before long he was connecting via modem to remote electronic forums known as bulletin boards to get free software and share code. He wrote an electronic book with a graphic interface, *Bulletin Board Bonanza*, explaining how to use bulletin boards and get online without paying connection fees. Posting it on electronic forums as shareware, he asked people to send donations if they found it useful. For $30, Mark would mail diskettes with handy software.

When checks and cash started showing up in his mailbox, Mark began promoting electronic books as a new marketing strategy. An e-book he created for chef Paul Prudhomme's Magic Seasoning Blends was featured in a special edition of *PC Computing* magazine as one of the top 100 free downloads on America Online, where he served as a moderator in the electronic publishing forum.

By the time Web browsers came along and the Internet took off, Mark was well ahead of the curve. As a designer and technology consultant, he applies aesthetic alchemy and technical know-how for clients including Travelocity, Mike's on the Avenue, French Quarter Suites and Beads by the Dozen. He is currently the Director of Internet Technologies for SPI Marketing, New York and the Webmaster of MardiGrasUnmasked.com. Using the latest technologies in clever ways is his forte.

"I'm manically creative," he says. "I can't help myself."

www.MardiGrasUnmasked.com
Mark@MardiGrasUnmasked.com

Graham Button

Graham was intently aiming his lens at Reggie Bush, atop a float in the Orpheus parade. A woman rider gesticulated urgently. What was she so worked up about? Couldn't she see that the guy with the camera, at this moment, was all about Reggie? Finally, Graham—*hel-lo*—got that she was trying to divert his attention.

Turning around—*whoa*! There's Sean Payton on the street, holding forth the Lombardi Trophy to parade goers lining the barricades. Grabbing the rock-star coach around the neck, an excited woman plants a fat kiss on his face. Love dat! Graham switches his camera to video mode and giddily rolls with the surreal fan-demonium. In this ecstatic moment, the blessings of the Saints seemed beyond comprehension. (Graham didn't realize it at the time, but his future *Black & Gold Party*

Gras colleague, Ray Broussard, was also right there, photographing many touches of the trophy.)

Based in San Francisco, Graham is self-employed as a freelance writer and wholesale distributor of sports- and event-related merchandise (mostly wearable regalia). His interest in event merchandising evolved out of an ongoing fascination with the history, culture and customs associated with holidays, celebrations and thematic events.

Graham's fateful indoctrination into New Orleans music and culture began at the Jazz & Heritage Festival, in 1989. A fascination with Mardi Gras started to take hold in 1994, and he subsequently profiled float builder Blaine Kern, aka Mr. Mardi Gras, for *Forbes* magazine. His first endeavor after leaving *Forbes* in 1996 was publishing a pocket fold-out guide to Mardi Gras, *The Mardi Card*. MardiCard.com launched in 1999 and eventually morphed into MardiGrasUnmasked.com, which has endured thanks to a respect for the wisdom of fools and the true spirit of the festivities: an optimistic and enduring human capacity for merriment and make-believe, for mirthful mockery and the creative indulgence of whimsy.

www.MardiGrasUnmasked.com
Graham@MardiGrasUnmasked.com

Ray Broussard

A native New Orleanian from Gentilly and a Saints fan since day one, Ray attended many games at the old Tulane Stadium. He never wore a Schwegmann bag on his head.

Ray works as a photographer for corporate clients, mostly in industrial environments and at corporate events. His favorite pastime is taking pictures of gatherings where New Orleanians are having a good time together: Mardi Gras, Jazz Fest, crawfish boils, non-funeral second lines, family get-togethers.

Shooting the Buddy D parade, Ray had a sense that something historic was developing and that the party was just beginning. Casual documentation was not an option.

In the street for Lombardi Gras without valid media credentials, Ray ran up and down the parade route like a mad man—dodging police, marching bands, floats and horse poop while trying to capture all the surreal, unique and beautiful scenes only possible in the Who Dat Nation.

Ray wasn't surprised when the championship celebration naturally evolved into a black-and-gold Mardi Gras attended by the happiest Who Dats imaginable. Having obsessively tried to capture all the fun, he hopes the imagery in this book adequately expresses just how wonderful we all felt (is that even possible?), while also helping others better understand how we live and how much we unconditionally love and appreciate our boys in black and gold. Ray salutes his family for supporting him in his arduous quest to bring this book to fruition, and for believing it would bring smiles to Saints fans for many years to come.

"Thanks to our Saints, we had the biggest party ever."

www.ByRayBroussard.com
Ray@ByRayBroussard.com

"It [the Saints winning the Super Bowl] meant no matter what adversity humans face, they can turn it around with hard work. It symbolized us picking ourselves up. I find it heroic. It just represents human nature at its best. That we can pick ourselves up when we're down. It's like the Book of Job. The Saints helped this city turn a great atrocity around by bringing people together. The Super Bowl in some way, I'm not exactly sure why, was about the human spirit prevailing."

—**Brad Pitt,** actor and New Orleans resident,
as quoted in the New Orleans *Times-Picayune*
(interview by historian Douglas Brinkley)